I0051763

Communication
Beyond Boundaries

Communication Beyond Boundaries

Payal Mehra

Communication Beyond Boundaries

Copyright © Business Expert Press, LLC, 2014.

All rights reserved. No part of this publication may be reproduced, stored in a retrieval system, or transmitted in any form or by any means—electronic, mechanical, photocopy, recording, or any other except for brief quotations, not to exceed 400 words, without the prior permission of the publisher.

First published in 2014 by
Business Expert Press, LLC
222 East 46th Street, New York, NY 10017
www.businessexpertpress.com

ISBN-13: 978-1-60649-638-1 (paperback)
ISBN-13: 978-1-60649-639-8 (e-book)

Business Expert Press Corporate Communication collection

Collection ISSN: 2156-8162 (print)
Collection ISSN: 2156-8170 (electronic)

Cover and interior design by Exeter Premedia Services Private Ltd., Chennai, India

First edition: 2014

10 9 8 7 6 5 4 3 2 1

Printed in the United States of America.

To my Father
holding on to your memories...

Abstract

This handy book on intercultural communication is ideal for the busy executive, frequent international business traveler, expatriate, and student of international business communication. It offers insights into the finer nuances of intercultural communication and assists in decision making, problem solving, and adjusting to other cultures. Lucid and practical in its approach, the book is replete with numerous examples that illustrate business beyond boundaries. It goes beyond a mere laundry list approach to one that enumerates the underlying phenomena that characterize international meetings, presentations, and negotiations. It offers a unique South Asian perspective on cross-cultural communication and is a must-read for those getting ready to sign international deals in the near future.

Keywords

assimilation, contexting, cross border merger and acquisitions, cultural communication frameworks, cultural intelligence, international business etiquette, international business negotiation, language, multicultural team development, speech acts, reasoning styles

Contents

Preface

This book brings together culture and communication beyond borders. It is specifically tailored to address the needs of business professionals working in diverse parts of the world, expatriates, frequent international business travelers, as well as students of international business communication.

As a teacher and a trainer, I have always felt the need for a concise book on intercultural communication rooted in practical aspects and geared toward learning on the job. Though the market is inundated with books on intercultural and cross-cultural communication, most of them are, to put it mildly, intellectual treatises on the theme. I also feel that the Asian viewpoint is missing from most of the textbooks; this book attempts to correct that.

This book aims to ensure usability, which is why it adopts a pragmatic approach to learning. It integrates both content as well as process. It uses stories from around the world to present the latest and most relevant concepts in intercultural communication. Written in a down-to-earth style, with the help of a broad array of engaging examples, the book illustrates how communication works and applies beyond traditional boundaries—geographic, personal, and psychological.

In creating this text, I am indebted to my series editor, Professor Debbie DuFrene, without whose painstaking editing, the book would not have been in its present form. Special thanks are due to Shyam Joseph, project manager, for giving the final shape to the book. I am especially thankful to my students whose enthusiasm toward the subject motivated me to write this book. My family is my life-support system; thank you, Sanjay, Rhea, and Aarushi for just being there.

I look forward to receiving feedback for improvements to future editions.

CHAPTER 1

Introducing Concepts

A closed mind is like a closed book, just a block of wood.
—Chinese proverb

Introduction

Dramatic changes in communication technology, transnational mergers and acquisitions, tourism, and even international study programs have increasingly contributed to the growing importance of cross border communication. Communication media, technology usage, decision-making norms, direct and indirect patterns of communication, content unfolding, and delivery methods are very much influenced by culture and business interests. These variations make communication strategy an absolute imperative in achieving business objectives.

Business is becoming a truly global enterprise. Recent trends indicate that the center of gravity in business is gradually shifting both economically as well as politically. Most developed countries are now looking eastward for global expansion. As the ratio of dependents to earners rises, the markets are getting flatter, traditional product offerings cease to be relevant, and developing countries are reaping the benefits of a demographic dividend. This shift necessitates a new worldview that is accommodative, adaptive, and adjusting. In the era of globalization, where geographic borders have gradually lost their traditional separating rigidity, intercultural communication abilities have become crucial for the survival and development of any company.

Globalization is a truism. To be truly global, not only must countries or companies globalize, but also individuals. It is individuals that communicate rather than businesses or organizations. Communication relies on continuous negotiation between individuals who interact in different social contexts to achieve specific goals. Communication is constantly shaped by perceptions that emanate from the cultural backgrounds of the individuals as well as their experiences. One's perception of everyday reality is, in truth, a complex collection of *intersecting frames* that transform otherwise meaningless experiences into meaningful interactions. *Framing* thus sets the individuals on a position of maximum awareness of their own behavior and appreciation of the others' reactions, confronting them with such concepts as standards, rules, and etiquette, all crucial for social integration and assertion. Framing is experience-based (What does the situation demand of me?), and involves the structuring of perception (How should I interact to resolve the issue?).

The field of business communication involves social intercourse, where there is a constant pressure of framing. This is enhanced by such stakes as professional prestige, relative position in the company hierarchy, and last but not least, financial incentive. Role-playing is more stringent as compared to regular social interaction because the norms of behavior are more rigid, and the people involved may not be strategically acting in the interest of the individual or the company. In a multinational company, these issues may get compounded because of the wide range of value systems involved.

To summarize, communication beyond boundaries involves expertise in the understanding of the complex web of cultural frames. Effective interchange yields a heterogeneous environment in which people belonging to diverse cultures and ethnicities achieve stated business objectives.

Understanding Culture

Cultural communication studies have been gaining in prominence. A review of intercultural literature and citation indexes suggest that the following scholarship has contributed immensely toward the study of intercultural communication at the global workplace. Edward Hall (1959) is credited with the introduction of a number of new concepts such as proxemics, polychromic and monochromic time, as well as contexting. Geert Hofstede (1980, 1983, and 1991) is best known for his cultural dimensions theory (concepts of power distance, individualism, uncertainty avoidance, masculinity, and long-term orientation). Shalom H. Schwartz propounded the concept of universal values (1994, 1999). The model of national culture differences with its seven key dimensions by Fons Trompenaars (1995) is often applied to general business and management. Cultural intelligence and ways to develop the same are highlighted in Christopher Earley and Soon Ang's book by the same name (2003).

Culture is a powerful force that shapes communication. Culture is like a mirror that reflects the perceptions with which one makes sense of the surroundings; it provides a framework to structure thoughts, actions, words and speech, as well as the language to express one's thought. It is thus a pattern of thought, a pattern of behavior, and a pattern of artifacts (symbols and products) that help individuals make sense of the world around them.

Two underlying processes shape the knowledge about one's own culture and the "other" culture. These processes are known as *enculturation* and *acculturation*. Enculturation is the process of classifying, coding, prioritizing, and justifying reality relative to the culture of one's origin. It is thus the culture handed down to the individual from the immediate social environment such as family, friends, the workplace, and so on. It includes values and beliefs derived from observation and experience. On the other hand, acculturation refers to the other culture and can involve four key processes: integration, separation, assimilation, and deculturation.

The immigrant, migrant, traveller, or expatriate may experience acculturation in these ways:

- *Integration*: The individual integrates into the new culture, at the same time being rooted to the culture of origin.
- *Separation*: The individual is separated from his or her new culture, even when living in the new culture.
- *Assimilation*: The individual assimilates into the new culture at the cost of the culture of origin.
- *Deculturation*: The individual is separated from his or her culture of origin as well as the new culture. The four processes of acculturation are summarized in Figure 1.1 in the following text.

Old culture

	Preserved	Separated
Absorbed	Integration	Assimilation
Separated	Separation	Deculturation

New Culture

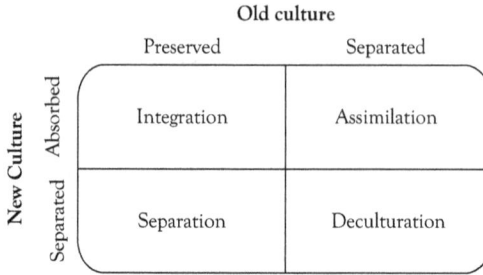

Figure 1.1 *Aspects of acculturation*

As people from different cultural groups start working together, cultural values can collide, resulting in misunderstandings and misgivings. Individuals can react unmindfully, which leads to derailment of the project and the partnerships. Oftentimes, those involved are unaware of cultural issues and that their cultural values divide them.

> People often fail to understand cultural issues. For example, an expatriate with four years' experience working in the retail sector in India was asked to discuss some of the cultural characteristics of Indians. He answered, "Well, they tend to be shorter than I am, their skin color is darker than mine, and they have black oily hair!"

Different Interpretations of Culture

Culture can be described in various ways:

1. Culture as food, music, love of poetry, folklore, drama, and literature.
2. Culture as history, monuments, religion, and ethics.
3. Culture as an adjective (for example, "The person is very cultured"), indicating courtesy, manners, and public deportment.
4. Culture as learned behavior: This approach takes into account the view of culture as action–behavior that is learned without adequate knowledge of the bases for these actions. This stereotypical view of culture focuses on laundry lists of dos and don'ts to be followed in a particular culture with respect to interactions such as negotiations, meetings, and presentations.

5. Culture as shared values: This approach considers culture as a set of inculcated values shared by all members of that community. The focus is on the thought processes that guide behavior or action. Thus, every culture has a set of values, a certain predisposition to behave in a particular way within a belief system. For instance, cultures can be direct or indirect in communication and monochromic or polychromic in time orientation.

6. Culture as tension between opposing values: This approach considers a culture to be a dynamic entity, which responds to external changes while simultaneously handling its own internal conflicts toward the change. The culture pursues a state of homeostasis while adjusting to external changes.

7. Culture as a system: This approach views culture as a complex interplay of factors that shape human behavior. These factors include the individual's personality, family values, religion, class, enculturation, and the social context (characteristics of the audience, institutional setting, the opponent's behavior in a negotiation context, etc.).

Academicians decidedly prefer the last approach as it helps to map complex behavior. However, practitioners benefit more from the fourth and the fifth approaches as these are predictive and help to establish the means for moving ahead.

Understanding Communication

Communication with others involves giving or receiving a message via a medium and anticipating the response of the other. When two people know each other, each individual is more confident of the reply. Otherwise, a state of eager anticipation is typical.

In terms of cross-cultural communication, communication with strangers often takes refuge in stereotyping. Stereotypes are usually inaccurate and not applicable to a particular individual. To improve communication with strangers, concentrate on the following processes:

1. Move from automatic to reflective responses: Immense conscious awareness about the self helps us differentiate an individual's core

intent from stereotypical categories. This calls for a global mindset that is tolerant, unprejudiced, and free from bigotry.

2. Learn how to deal with unfamiliar scripts: Much of the day-to-day communication focuses on familiar scripts and these can be unreliable when communicating with a stranger. This calls for a flexible attitude and an "elastic mentality" that accepts differences and embraces similarities.

Communication Beyond Familiar Boundaries

Communication beyond familiar boundaries takes place at three levels.

- *Level 1*: The cultural level, which involves collecting information about another culture's dominant norms, etiquettes, communication styles, and its values and beliefs
- *Level 2*: The sociocultural level, which involves collecting information about the dominant group or the subgroup to which the members of the other culture belong
- *Level 3*: The psychocultural level, which involves collecting information about the characteristics of the individual of the other culture as distinct from the group to which he or she belongs or the culture of origin

Experts also address the following three levels of cultural intelligence.

1. *The cognitive level.* In this first stage, the person familiarizes himself or herself with the norms about the other culture on the surface level. This is at a superficial level. Information is gleaned from various sources. The approach is focused on the "front stage" part of culture.
2. *The behavioral level.* In this second level, the person acts out the expected behavior based on an understanding that stems from reading and observing.
3. *The emotional level.* This deeper level involves empathy, knowing the *why* of certain unfamiliar customs and acquainting oneself with the backstage part of the culture.

Cultural intelligence will be discussed in detail in a later chapter.

Commonly Misused Cultural Terms

Three frequently used terms are intercultural communication, cross-cultural communication, and international business communication.

Intercultural Communication

In its most basic form, intercultural communication is an academic field of study that seeks to understand how people from different cultures behave, interact, and perceive the world around them. This definition supposes that it is not cultures that communicate, but individuals belonging to those cultures. Cultures could be people belonging to different nationalities, subgroups, ethnic groups, religious groups, and so on. Findings are then applied to real-life situations such as intercultural negotiations, advertising, website design, and meetings in business. Intercultural communication is essentially multidisciplinary in nature and borrows from social sciences such as anthropology, sociology, psychology, and communication studies. Edward T. Hall, Geert Hofstede, Harry C. Triandis, Fons Trompenaars, Clifford Geertz, and Shalom Schwartz are noted researchers on intercultural communication.

With more and more businesses going global, companies need to know how best to organize the structure of their companies, manage diverse staff, and communicate with global clients and customers. Intercultural communication provides much-needed expertise and enables the companies to respond effectively to markets, suppliers, and clients.

Cross-Cultural Communication

The term intercultural is often confused with the largely synonymous term cross-cultural communication. While the phrase *intercultural communication* is a study, cross-cultural communication is a skill and describes the ability to successfully form relationships with members of other cultures. This is achieved through the process of exchange of information, skillful persuasion, masterful mediation, and the creation and the sharing of meaning through language, gestures, proxemics, oculesics, and others. It is a skill that is practiced through continuous learning, reading, interactions, and so on.

International Business Communication

International business communication is communication that occurs across international borders, that is, nations defined by geographic frontiers. It is traditionally concerned with government-to-government exchanges. Often, agenda is dictated by the most powerful nations.

Two constructs stand out in the study of culture—the *emic* and the *etic*. Emic focuses on the ethnic viewpoint (the specific or the stereotypical approach), while etic focuses on the cross-cultural point of view (the generalist or the more expansive approach). Generalizations about cultures allow comparisons to be made as new information is organized into mental categories. Stereotypes are oversimplified images of a person or culture. Stereotypes differ from mental categories because they are inflexible and not open to new information.

Multicultural Versus Ethnocentric Managers

People who can easily move, adapt to the other cultures, and feel comfortable in all types of surroundings are said to be multicultural in orientation and personality. These managers

- work effectively with many cultural groups;
- concentrate on the similarities rather than the differences between their team members to get work done;
- have a global mindset;
- know (intuitively or otherwise) what motivates individuals with different cultural backgrounds;
- do not judge or evaluate others;
- appreciate that people have different values, beliefs, and approaches to perform tasks related to business;
- understand that decision making is a joint effort.

People who have a rigid belief that their way of doing work is the best way and resist opposition to their work view are said to be ethnocentric in orientation and personality. These managers

- are comfortable with members of their community only;
- focus on individual differences;
- have a provincial mindset;
- know what motivates themselves only;
- judge and evaluate others easily using self-reference criteria;
- are task focused.

Experiencing Culture on the Job: Impact on Communication

Communication styles differ from culture to culture. Even within the same culture, one can find variations. The so-called Indian culture is, in fact, a potpourri of many subcultures; 122 languages, of which 22 languages are spoken by over 1 million people, while the remaining 100 languages are spoken by more than 10,000 people, and over 1,500 "mother tongues" are used in India (Census India 2010–2011); and widely differing rituals varying from one region to another.

There is no one African culture or society, as it exists in many people's mind. Africa is vast, comprising 54 independent nations, 1.02 billion people, and over 3,000 ethnic groups speaking more than 1,000 indigenous languages—in addition to the six European languages (French, English, Portuguese, German, Spanish, and Italian) carried over from prior colonization. Sub-Saharan Africa is culturally complex and commonly referred to as "black" Africa. Certainly, they share many cultural backgrounds that have been carried for centuries, but with enormous variations. For example, Congo is not Togo and Togo is not Rwanda; those differences exist not only among countries but within countries as well. These common beliefs and core cultural values transcend national boundaries, languages, and ethnicities and form a fundamental cultural unit. It is vital that expatriate managers have a basic knowledge of cross-cultural differences and affiliations between countries.

In terms of working in a different cultural setup or with people of different nationalities, it is helpful to seek answers to the following questions.

How Important Are Relationships in Getting the Job Done?

Some cultures pride themselves on relationship building and preserving harmony at all costs. These are indirect communicators who value processes over the result or the outcome. These cultures place a high premium on establishing a relationship early on in the collaboration. For instance, the Europeans, particularly the Germans, Swiss, and the Americans tend to initially concentrate on the assigned task and let relationship development take its own natural time, while the Asians (such as the Japanese, the Thais, and the Chinese) attach more value to relationship building at the start of the project, believing that this would lead to better task performance at the end. This does not imply that any of the cultures are less committed to the task at hand; it is just that they pursue it differently.

What Is the Approach to Teamwork?

In a multicultural or a global team, the culture of origin may determine the individual's approach to teamwork. Other determinants include gender, emotional and cognitive intelligences, shared experiences, and personality. Some cultures are more individualistic than others (American), while some are collectivist in orientation (Indian). In some cultures, dissent and debates are encouraged (Germany); in others, saving face is critical (Taiwan).

Culture affects to a large extent how members visualize their role, responsibilities, and contribution in a team. A few cultures lay a high premium on hierarchy (India), whereas others focus more on delegation and empowerment. The hierarchical cultures are deferential to authority as well as seniority of both age and position. This could be due to the social structure, which values high power distance.

Cultures also differ on norms of decision making. In some cultures, decisions are totally decentralized; in others, the approval of the higher-ups is required to be taken for even routine transactions, managing conflicts, brainstorming, and even day-to-day management activities. Some cultures are painstakingly formal (Germany), while others are way too informal in their approach.

How Is Time Emphasized?

Some cultures are monochromic, that is, they have a strict sense of time (United States, Germany). Others are polychromic, in that their sense of timing is inferred from the context and the surroundings (some African countries, Mexico, India). This impacts communication as the latter are more relaxed and usually operate from a different mindset than those who are rigid about deadlines. Unlike the polychromes, the monochromes are well planned, meticulous, and at ease using personal digital assistants (PDAs) or other time management devices. Effective at multitasking, they would feel uncomfortable socializing with business colleagues after office hours.

How Direct Are the Lines of Communication?

Is it easy to talk to the top management or does one have to follow proper communication channels? In some cultures—such as India, China, Japan, and Thailand—position, power, and authority are highly valued attributes. It is difficult to communicate disagreement to the superiors in these cultures. Conversely, some cultures like the Dutch and the Germans almost expect dissent. It is customary to speak up in these cultures for fear of being misconstrued as unproductive and a "wallpaper" during meetings. As compared to the southern European counterparts, northern Europe has a lower power distance index, which is correct in the cultural context from which they come.

Do Differences Exist with Regard to Low-Context and High-Context Communication Styles?

Context refers to the circumstances that form the setting of an event, an idea, or a situation, which form a backdrop to the current task or transaction at hand. It presents a rationale and logic to fully grasp and understand the event so that the same may be successfully executed.

The United States is characterized by a low-context culture and has a direct communication style. This is characterized by a deductive approach to communication where emphasis is primarily on facts and evidence supporting the end result, which is stated upfront. It assumes that too little of the context is unknown; consequently, the culture expects detailed instructions to reduce anxiety and uncertainty in transactions. Other cultures that fall into this category are the Swiss, Germans, Finns, Dutch, and Norwegians. The overriding purpose of communication is to exchange and share information with each other to facilitate task fulfillment.

India is characterized by a high-context culture and has an indirect communication style. This is characterized by an inductive approach where the emphasis is on the background (history or the backdrop), opinions and inferences leading to the conclusion, and the end result. It assumes that much of the context is already known; consequently, the culture expects the broad picture to follow through investigation. Much emphasis is on what is not said, and messages are understood by one's ability to read between the lines. The full impact of the message is inferred from the body language, gestures, and the facial expression of the communicators. In these cultures, people also try to convey meaning by changing the context. Japan, the Middle East, Thailand, and some European countries such as Italy are other examples of high-context cultures. The overriding purpose of communication is to maintain harmony and peace as a means to successfully complete a task.

Is the Communication Style Linear or Circular?

In a linear communication style, messages are organized around tasks, outcomes, and processes. Linear communicators speak directly and to the point. They speak frankly and at times may be perceived as blunt and aggressive. In the linear style, small talk proceeds after the main business is completed, unlike the circular style of communication.

A circular communication styles is indirect. These communicators value harmony and courtesy. They seek out polite responses from the audience. They prefer silence to dissent and often avoid giving bad news directly. They usually leave the sentence half finished and appear to be hesitant in expressing a firm opinion. Meanings are embedded in eye

> An Indian expatriate reporting to his Argentinean boss once received this feedback from him: "The problem with Indians is that they know too much English….You speak too much, in a roundabout way, using lots of jargon, that makes listening and understanding so difficult. Why don't you just explain to me using *key words*...?"

contact, gestures, and facial expression. These types of communicators are prone to using repetition, adjectives, flowery language, and storytelling to convey their message.

Is the Culture a "We"-Type or an "I"-Type Culture?

A "we"-type culture emphasizes group decision making over personal delegation and elevation of a single individual to the top position. Some companies encourage competitiveness and cutthroat behavior from employees. Others emphasize family values over career goals and aspirations. In some companies, there are no hierarchies, while in others many levels of decision making exist. This impacts communication on the job as well. "We"-type people use words that emphasize team efforts as against the "I"-type people who stress individual achievement over group achievement. Use of "I" indicates individualism, delegation of authority, and self-promotion for career goals. Use of "we" indicates collectivism, group decision making, and team achievement.

What Are the Information-Gathering Processes?

The western world focuses extensively on data collection, sorting, and categorization for any meaningful results to emerge. In contrast, some eastern and African cultures would be less concerned with the spreadsheet and the array of numbers, believing that a general approach must be adopted first to truly understand the issue. Some groups learn to look at data separately from its surrounding context, while others value data as an integrated part of the whole. Some cultures like to evaluate the statistical information in a step-by-step manner; others like to set up strategic teams to discuss the big picture.

How is Language Used in Business?

The universally accepted language of business is the English language though it is not used universally. Some countries such as France take pride in their language and do not encourage the use of English. A few nations feel insulted by the assumption that English would be used as a means of communication in the business discourse. Problems are compounded when one or more partners do not speak a common language; the local language can then influence the dynamics of translation. Language thus becomes a barrier to communication rather than an enabler especially in an international context.

The French culture ministry has stopped the usage of some English words in the French lexicon. In 2008, popular terms such as *e-mail, blog, fast food, supermodel, takeaway, low-cost airline, shadowboxing,* and *detachable motor caravan* were included in the 65 pages of banned words on the ministry's new website, which was launched that year. The report says that French linguists at the Academie Francaise—the body that monitors and protects the French language—have suggested Gallic equivalents to more than 500 mostly English words for the website, being run by the culture ministry's General Commission for Terminology. These include:

iPod	diffusion pour baladeur
Wi-Fi	acces sans fil a l'internet
Blog	bloc
Web	toile d'araignee mondiale
Multifunctional industrial buildings	batiment industriel polyvalent
Rise pipes	colonne montante
Coach	coup de pied de coin
Hashtag	mot-diese (this was added recently in January 2013).

Source: Simon (2013) and "France protects itself from the dreaded English language by banning 'fast-food' and 'podcasting'" (2013).

The language of business is different from the language used in social settings. It is more direct, more formal than the language used in social or even family settings. It is conservative and formal. Abusive language and swear words are not acceptable in a business setup. In comparison to face-to-face communication, written communication is treated as more businesslike and more often than not written contracts are binding on both the parties. Emotional expressions, use of flowery words, and adjectives are used minimally; emphasis is usually on more businesslike talk and signed deals. In spite of such awareness, variations do exist with respect to the culture of the organization, country, and that of the person. In many organizations and cultures, letters, contracts, proposals, and reports are worded using phrases selected carefully by the legal department of that organization. In other cultures, such particularity may not exist. Communication is rooted in the context and the audience; the language used for customers, clients, colleagues, bosses, and vendors will be quite different.

English phrases	American phrases
To table an item: Place on the table for discussion by everyone	To table an item: To put it away and close the discussion
Please use the lift	Please use the elevator
Put this in the boot	Put this in the trunk
Chemist	Drugstore
Solicitor	Lawyer
Passed	Graduated
Petrol	Gas
Bath	Shower
Bill	Check
Post	Mail
Pub	Bar

Does the Type of Firm Impact Communication on the Job?

A few sectors such as the advertising division tend to have a more relaxed dress code in comparison to others. Others service sectors like hospitality, for example, and consulting, financial, and legal businesses expect that the employees always stay well-dressed and formal. Traditional business expects more data for information processing for decision making than, for example, dot-com firms. Informally structured firms are more heuristic in their approach than businesses with a very formal organizational system.

How Do People Deal with Conflicts?

Conflicts are encouraged in some cultures as a means of self-expression. France, Germany, and even the United States are some of the countries that view conflict as a positive thing. Face-to-face discussions are encouraged to sort out differences and smooth relationships. In many countries such as China, Japan, Indonesia, and Taiwan, open conflicts are demeaning and a source of embarrassment. Face-to-face discussions are considered disruptive; issues may be sorted out through the written medium of communication.

What Are the Approaches Toward Disclosure?

In some cultures, people are uncomfortable about revealing too much. Emotions are kept in check especially when there has been a misunderstanding. They conceal their feelings and opinions about a person or an event unless it is absolutely necessary to reveal the facts about the same. Many cultures see no objection in revealing the facts about a case as objectively as possible. They do not consider this as an intrusion of their privacy.

How Do People Gain Knowledge?

Some cultures acquire knowledge through a systematic cognitive process of gathering data, evaluating the data, and predicting something with the help of that data. The data could be a secondary data or a primary data. Other cultures emphasize that knowledge can be obtained through reading and discussions. In some cultures, questions are asked to acquire more information (German, Swiss, and American). In others, questions are asked to confirm something that is already known (as in China, Japan, and India).

Summary

1. Business is becoming a truly global enterprise. Dramatic changes in communication technologies, cross border mergers and acquisitions, tourism, and even international study programs have increasingly contributed to the growing importance of cross border communication.
2. Culture is a powerful force that shapes communication.
3. Communication is manifested in the way culture reveals itself in the workplace. Culture is revealed through approaches toward time, proxemics, reporting structures and patterns, use of silence, and direct and indirect patterns of reporting.
4. Communication with strangers often takes refuge in stereotyping. A more effective way is to focus on generalizations relying more on one's intuition and personal experience.
5. Adaptation, assimilation, and adjustment are three key skills needed to succeed in business.

Key Terms

- Culture
- Communication
- Enculturation
- Acculturation (integration, separation, assimilation, deculturation)
- Intercultural communication
- Cross-cultural communication
- International communication
- Stereotype
- Generalization
- Cultural intelligence
- Ethnocentric
- Multicultural

CHAPTER 2

Cultural Frameworks and Communication Styles

What gives man his identity no matter where he is born—is his culture, the total communication framework: words, actions, postures, gestures, tones of voice, facial expressions, the way he handles time, space, and materials, and the new way he works, plays, makes love, and defends himself.

—Edward Hall, 1976

Introduction

The western hegemony is now greatly diminished. The economic order is inclined toward a multipolar equilibrium. The emerging power centers include countries such as China, India, Brazil, South Korea, South Africa, and Turkey. Revolutionary changes in technology, trade, investment, and migration have hastened the speed of globalization; yet these have created effects similar to a cultural deglobalization. Critics of globalization prefer to call the process internationalization as if the frontiers of countries would never be dissolved. People are now more anxious to resist cultural imperialism and preserve their roots. Cultural pluralism has replaced homogeneity even as popular global brands (McDonald, Pepsi, Coca-Cola, Apple, Nokia, Samsung, LG, KFC, and others) make their foray into the developing countries. Some brands are forced to localize to remain relevant in these new and emerging markets.

Global restaurant chains such as Kentucky Fried Chicken (KFC), McDonalds, and Subway are also offering *Jain* foods along with vegetarian foods in the largely vegetarian state of Gujarat in western

India. Subway has recently launched a pure *Jain* counter in Ahmedabad. KFC has also changed its menu to accommodate vegetarian cuisine.

Source: Unnithan (2013).

As business environment expands to accommodate different cultures, learning to communicate and transact business beyond boundaries has become even more critical. The cultural frameworks and models presented in the following text can help leaders and organizations share and develop critical insights as they prepare to cross-cultural and geographic boundaries.

Cultural models are frameworks that compare the similarities and differences between two or more cultures on certain international variables. International variables can be objective and easy-to-research data (such as political and economic systems, formatting systems for time, etc.) or they can be subjective (such as behavioral norms and value systems of the people). Cultural modeling has several advantages (Hoft 1998). The models help to

- identify information necessary for internationalization;
- understand cultural metaphors in a given context;
- evaluate the degree of localization or adaptation necessary;
- prevent visitors, tourists, and others from making any cultural *faux pas*.

Contexting and Communication Styles

Edward T. Hall (May 16, 1914–July 20, 2009), an anthropologist and a researcher on cross-cultural issues, pioneered the concept of low-context and high-context culture. He is also credited with introducing new concepts such as proxemics, highlighted in his second book *The Hidden Dimension* (Hall, 1966), and polychromic and monochromic time orientations, described in his book *The Silent Language* (Hall, 1959).

Hall evolved a concept called the Primary Message Systems, which is a systematic method for observing and comparing cultures. In 1976, Hall developed the *iceberg analogy* of culture. He reasoned that each culture has a few visible aspects, as well as a larger portion, which is hidden beneath the surface. The tip of the iceberg is the behavior that is visible to all; the underlying reasons for the behavior (beliefs and thought patterns that underlie behavior) are below the surface and need to be tapped for better understanding of the thought processes and reasoning patterns of the particular society.

The iceberg theory proposes that individuals communicate from the conscious and the subconscious level. Much of the external manifestation of behavior (the visible part) is dependent on the internal thought processes. These thought processes in turn are shaped by personal as well as shared experiences, belief systems, and the culture of origin. While behavior is easier to change, values are more immutable and static. Much depends on the way one assimilates objective as well as subjective knowledge to achieve greater understanding of the self and others.

The iceberg model is important because it explains that we cannot judge a new culture based on only what we see when we merely observe or are initially introduced to it. We can truly understand a culture only when we stay in the culture, interact with the inhabitants, and immerse ourselves in it.

Contexting

Context refers to how much one needs to know before communicating effectively. A high-context communication style is one in which much of the context is known; meaning is embedded in the surrounding context. Norms are largely understood through an unwritten code of conduct. This is in contrast to the low-context communication style in which the meaning is in the message, and very little is assumed or taken for granted. The rules are explicit; therefore, the communication is direct and clear.

This concept has important business implications. The Swiss, Germans, and Americans are low-context communicators; in their culture, their rules and guidelines are detailed and clearly spelled out. For them, a contract (the written word) is sacrosanct. Extrovert and outgoing, these people communicate exuberantly with vigor and dynamism. Most people from cultures typified by a low-context communication style come quickly to the point. They are task oriented and do not indulge in insignificant small talk early in the collaboration.

The Chinese, Koreans, Arabs, and Japanese are high-context communicators; in their cultures, it is the nonverbal signs, gestures, and facial expressions that reveal much of the message. Introvert and reserved in their demeanor (especially the Chinese, Koreans, and Japanese), their reactions are inwardly directed rather than publicly expressed. Most cultures representing high-context communication style take some time to come to the point. Nonconfrontationist and relationship centered, they value small talk conducted over dinner and entertainment as a key to understanding the other person. In their business activity, a contract is merely a starting point. It may be modified to suit individual interests later on.

However, it should be said that individuals can be both high context as well as low context in their behavior. For instance, a person may be high context in relationships with friends and family and low context in business scenarios. In some countries traditionally considered high context, such as India, communication is becoming increasingly low context due to the influence of Internet technologies and globalization.

What Do Direct and Indirect Communicators Think of Each Other?

Communicators with a particular context orientation often share common beliefs about the other group.

Direct communicators think that indirect communicators

- evade the real issue;
- are not honest in their intentions;
- are too subservient to authority;
- tend to procrastinate;
- focus too much on superficialities.

Indirect communicators think that direct communicators

- are tactless;
- are too practical in their approach;
- lack empathy;
- focus only on the task at hand;
- are rude.

Differences Between Low-Context and High-Context Communicators

The following generalizations apply to low-context and high-context communicators:

Low-context communicators use a direct, confrontational, and explicit approach. On the other hand, a person from a high-context culture will rarely refer to a problem directly; the message would evolve from the context or the reference to the background. People from this cultural setup avoid confrontationist language, preferring to let the nonverbal communication speak for itself. It is left to the listener to grasp the meaning from the context.

If a North American heading a consultant firm was unhappy with the proposal submitted by the Indian principal consultant, he would directly express his displeasure over the language, structure, and research content in no uncertain terms. In contrast, an Indian would say something like "I appreciate the hard work that you have put into the report; however, I feel that we could work more on the research. What do you think about the formatting? Also do you think you need to review the language as well?" Indians tend to be wordy in their communication, often being verbose to the extent of obfuscation.

Low-context communicators rely on explicit signs and signals. A low-context country (such as Germany, United States, and Sweden) is characterized by an abundance of signs and signals to guide the traveler. There are signs to direct one to the taxi stand, the next station, or elevator, and to tourist information and transportation offices. All the streets have names and numbers prominently displayed. In contrast, everybody seems to know where to go in a high-context country (such as India, Pakistan, and China). There is little information available to aid understanding of routes and traffic schedules.

Low-context communicators regulate behavior through written norms and codes of conduct. In India, rules exist with respect to application for leave. However, leave is usually negotiated between the employee and his boss, rather than availed as a right. The employee will cite various reasons for the leave such as a close family wedding, death of a close family member, and so on. The request is granted at the personal discretion of the boss. Moreover, the employee on leave has to be available on the mobile phone or e-mail. This is in contrast to the situation in a New York office. Managers who need a few days to a week off follow the personnel manual to know whether they are entitled to a holiday. They will not likely feel as obligated to justify the need for the requested leave but will request the boss's approval of the selected days of absence.

Low-context communicators enforce compliance through contracts. In China, the contract is perceived to be the starting point of building a connection or *guanxi*. In most high-context countries, a contract is just a preliminary agreement, which may be modified to suit changing conditions. In low-context countries, a contract is a detailed document outlining every aspect of the transaction. It incorporates clauses to deal with all kinds of contingencies. The contract is fixed and immutable; violations are dealt with in the court of law. In high-context countries, it is not perceived to be necessary to put everything in writing, as the primary focus of a transaction is relationship building. In low-context countries, the contract defines the relationships; the primary purpose is to establish the agreement to do business.

Low-context communicators negotiate forcefully. During negotiations, people belonging to countries such as the United States, Germany, and Australia are more forceful in their demeanor as compared to their high-context counterparts such as the Japanese, Chinese, Taiwanese, and Indonesians. While a yes is a definite affirmative for most westerners, it may not hold true for Asians. Yes can mean maybe, not sure, or even no. If the proposal is not up to the mark, Asians may avoid giving very direct responses—We will look into it, We will consider it, and We will reply to this soon—are ways to indicate acknowledgment of the proposal. The Japanese also resort to long periods of silences to indicate displeasure or disagreement.

The reason why Asians prefer to be indirect in conveying bad news is to save face (their own or that of the others) and to avoid personal conflicts and disturbance of harmony in relationships. Westerners on the other hand tend to be more frank and direct. They distrust silences and feel that it is wrong to hide the truth in the garb of relationship building, deference, and courtesy. They believe in forceful arguments, data-filled reports, lengthy calculations, and strong visuals to explain the logic. The underlying reason for these noted differences in meeting behavior results from the purposes meetings serve in different cultures. In low-context cultures, meetings are essentially conducted to arrive at important decisions. Participants are expected to express their views and opinions freely in the meeting. In high-context cultures, meetings are usually a forum for groupthink; leaders use this platform to announce decisions to the employees of the company. Deliberations and decision making are behind the scenes and usually at higher levels. Haggling and bargaining are considered the norm.

Low-context cultures are less relationship based and more rule based. Rule-based cultures (such as United States, Australia, Germany, Switzerland, Sweden, United Kingdom, Netherlands, Czech Republic, Slovakia, Belgium, and France), also labeled *universalists* by researcher Trompenaars, are primarily determined by codes of conduct explicitly laid down in the rule book. Compliance is enforced not by fear or guilt but by what is legally permissible and not permissible. The social and cultural norms of behavior are therefore explicit in the communication. The frank nature of the Western society stems from an innate confidence in the rule of law. There are certain absolutes that are applicable to everybody regardless of the situation or the person involved. In contrast, authority in high-context cultures (such as Brazil, Italy, Turkey, Japan, Argentina, India, Pakistan, Mexico, and Thailand) resides in parents, seniors, leaders, and elders. Relationships and behavior are regulated through close supervision by these authority figures who constitute the in-group that differs from the wider community (the out groups). Behavior that does not conform to the norms and standards results in shame, loss of face, punishment, and even ostracism from the group, community, or society. The social and cultural norms are implicit in the communication. Labeled as *particularists* by Trompenaars, these societies treat everybody as unique with their own set of problems and issues.

Asians find it quite strange that children in the United States and Sweden can complain against their parents and that the parents can be tried in a court of law for violation of children's rights. Westerners on the other hand, find it difficult to accept that in India a significant majority cannot marry without their parents' consent.

Low-context cultures believe in greater transparency. Western-style management places a high premium on transparency, which means that information is made publicly available. This is especially true in financial and investment dealings. Eastern-style dealings are focused more on personal connections. The balance sheet, profit and loss statements, and annual reports are regulated by the law to ensure transparency and adherence to intricate reporting standards. This is not to suggest that one is superior to the other, for both the systems have their pros and cons. Relationship-based trust building takes time, but it may be highly stable in periods of economic turmoil.

Cultural Differences in Expectations for Disclosure and Transparency

Example 1:

Little did Indian Rajat Gupta, former director of Goldman Sachs Group Inc., imagine the trouble he would encounter with the U.S. legal system for his indiscretion. He passed on privileged information to his friend Raj Rajaratnam, cofounder of the hedge fund management firm, Galleon Group LLC. Goldman Sachs considered the action a criminal offense and claimed that, as a result of Gupta's crimes, it was entitled to $6.9 million in legal fees and other expenses it had spent during a federal probe of the bank by the Manhattan U.S. Attorney's Office and the Federal Bureau of Investigation, as well as a parallel investigation by the U.S. Securities and Exchange Commission. Gupta was ordered to pay the bank more than $6.2 million in restitution for his insider trading.

Example 2:

During the aftermath of the Tohuku earthquake and tsunami in March 2011 causing the Fukushima nuclear tragedy, the Japanese received widespread criticism for the way in which the crisis was handled. They were accused by the Western media for withholding information and denying the facts related to the incident. Prime Minister Kan was quoted by the press as calling for calm and understating accounts of the tragedy. Political analyst, Dean Henderson, notes a historical pattern for this behavior, which traces its roots to the patriarchal influence of the Emperor, so much that the Japanese rarely question their leaders. Over a period of time, they have learned to suppress their feelings.

Source: Henderson (2012).

Low-context cultures tend to be less bureaucratic than high-context cultures. A research reports that once the U.S. government required the filling of approximately 26 forms for the approval of a joint venture in 9 administrative procedures. For a similar type of venture, Japan required 325 documents to be filled in 46 administrative procedures and South Korea required 312 documents to be filled in 62 administrative procedures (De Mente 1995). In India, the situation is even worse. Single-window clearances rarely exist, and corruption may slow down the business process even further. To minimize corrupt practices, Dubai has two options for the applicant. In the first, the applicant can follow the due process of law with a lower fee and longer processing times. The second option offers the applicant the benefit of a shorter processing time albeit with a higher processing fee.

Low-context communicators demonstrate less deference than the high-context communicators. High-context communicators display a significant amount of courtesy in business. Formality and politeness are highly regarded in business as a form of respect to seniors and group members. In some cultures (such as Korea), age is to be respected. Respect is demonstrated by giving gifts, addressing people with their titles (Sir, My Lord), and even through body language. In Japan, bows and lowered eyes indicate deference as do both hands clasped in front. In Middle Eastern countries such as Saudi Arabia, crossing of legs is offensive as is passing on something to someone with the left (or the unclean) hand. In some countries (such as Japan), the giving and receiving of the business card is also deeply ritualistic. A card must be taken with both hands and not placed in the pocket without first reading what is written on it.

Low-context communicators are associated with low uncertainty avoidance cultures. Uncertainty avoidance refers to the level of tolerance of ambiguity and uncertainty. It indicates the extent to which people are comfortable in relatively unstructured circumstances. Cultures low on uncertainty avoidance (Germany and United States to some extent) attempt to minimize uncertainty by creating rules and regulations to control the same. These cultures also have a low-context communication style. In contrast, cultures high on uncertainty avoidance (India, Japan, Singapore, China, and Turkey) are also high-context communicators. They are uncertainty tolerant and adaptive toward changing circumstances.

Low-context cultures market brands and services differently. With regard to business-to-business (B2B) marketing, the way Westerners network is very different from the activities of the eastern world. In the West, networking is a professional concept often developed over a business lunch or at a trade fair. It is typically focused on cultivating relationships for future gains. In contrast, the relationship-based cultures network extensively through preestablished connections often extending to friends and family.

Differences Within Low-Context Cultures

Business communication styles can differ markedly even among the rule-based cultures. The following scenarios demonstrate the difference:

1. In a presentation to a German firm, the American supplier started with a humorous anecdote to break the ice. However, this was not well received by the Germans. Germans appreciate seriousness and professionalism during meetings and presentations. They regard jokes as casual behavior and prefer graphs and charts to the flashy phrases that Americans tend to use in their presentations.
2. In a meeting with a Scandinavian firm, Americans used tough aggressive language peppered with sports analogies. This was not favorable to the Scandinavians who prefer a softer, matter-of-fact approach in their business meetings.
3. In a meeting among the British, Italian, and the French business people, the French would be the frankest of the three; the Italian would tend to be the most voluble, while the British would be the most subtle.
4. Russians feel uncomfortable with foreigners and do not open up to people easily. They need business partners to reassure them about their seriousness and intent.
5. The U.S. Midwest is more low context than the U.S. Southeast.

Differences Within High-Context Cultures

Relationship-based cultures differ among themselves as the following examples suggest:

1. Pakistan has a purely male-dominated society where very little recognition is accorded to the female segment of the society. Mostly consisting of a tribal setup, the Pakistani society is run by norms and traditions set by men. The religion of Islam also provides men with enormous power to make all decisions about women's involvement in society. Decisions regarding education, marriage, work, and travel of women are made by their male family members. Pakistanis don't like to discuss their women in public, and gender equality and women's rights are commonly perceived as Western efforts to undermine their society. This behavior is in contrast to that of Turkey and Indonesia, countries that have a large majority of Muslims, but who have democratic principles in place and accommodate women in social and political life.

2. Those from China and Japan may be similar in concepts relating to face saving and relationship building. However, the Chinese are more direct in their communication than are the Japanese.

3. While the United Arab Emirates is an Islamic country, its citizens are more direct and rule based than those from Saudi Arabia, for example.

Monochromic and Polychromic Cultures

According to Edward Hall (1960), people belonging to a monochromic culture are very particular about time and tend to do one thing at a time. In contrast, polychromic people can multitask effectively and are less particular about time and punctuality. Normally, rule-based cultures are more monochromic than relationship-based cultures. Those in monochromic cultures

- believe time is money;
- structure their time in a systematic manner;

- view time as linear and compartmentalized (seconds, minutes, and hours);
- interpret the future as a definite time frame—two years, five years, or a maximum of 10 years;
- set future plans that are firm, organized, and quantified;
- set aside a time slot for each activity;
- make frequent to-do lists;
- view breaks and personal time as sacrosanct, though technology has caused blurring of work and personal time;
- are disciplined about time schedules and appointments.

The typical American businessperson usually purchases a round-trip ticket for business travel. This may backfire in cyclical time cultures such as that of China and Japan where people like to spend considerable time on negotiations. Mexicans, Indians, and Italians also have a more relaxed interpretation of time management, being largely polychromic cultures.

Polychromic and monochromic tendencies may be deciphered by the following: If you like to strictly observe queues, carry personal digital assistants (PDAs), planners, and calendars with you, and are uncomfortable with multitasking, you definitely have a monochromic tendency.

In contrast, those in polychromic cultures

- are less particular about structuring the task;
- consider time as being nonlinear and not segmented (seconds, minutes, and hours);
- can easily switch from one task to another;
- view the future as vague and undefined—the future can mean 10 years, 20 years, or even longer;
- do not fix, quantify, and schedule their future;
- use time management to regulate relationships;
- regard breaks and personal time as subordinate to relationships;
- are flexible with appointments and schedules.

India can be characterized as a polychromic culture, but punctuality is expected especially in business dealings. Subordinates typically show up on time to ensure that the boss is not kept waiting; bosses may arrive late to avoid loss of face as a result of waiting or simply to denote status and rank. Typical excuses for tardiness include being held up in traffic, personal problems, and medical emergencies. Indians also like to do some of their personal work during working hours such as depositing and withdrawing money from the bank, depositing fees for their children in school, attending parent–teacher meetings, and so on.

Some cultures are also characterized as cyclical with respect to how time is viewed. Cyclical cultures view time as a circular entity and allow events to unfold in a natural manner. In fact in these cultures (such as the Kenyan culture or the rural subgroup in India), it is the event that decides the time of the day rather than vice versa. Connection, trust, and linkages form the core of such cultures and affect their transactions. People frequently refer to the past and take a long time to deliberate on key issues. They tend to revisit issues again and again (in a cyclical manner) until they are satisfied that the correct decision is made.

Edward Hall, in his book *The Silent Language*, associated a high-context culture with a polychromic view of time. According to him, Latin American, Asian, Middle Eastern, and some Latin European countries are both high context as well as polychromic (Hall 1959).

A hotelier of German origin working in Saudi Arabia has now gotten used to the Arab culture of keeping visitors waiting beyond the appointed hour. He knows and understands now that Arabs do not say a no directly and tend to be doing a number of things simultaneously while in a meeting (attending to other calls on the mobile phone, signing papers, talking to another person, etc.). He patiently waits for his turn and relaxes while the Arabs attend to their other businesses.

Individualism and Collectivism

How people regard the *self* with respect to the community forms the basis of the key difference between collectivist and individualistic cultures. The dimension was proposed by Geert Hofstede (1980). Hofstede consulted for IBM during the late 1960s and early '70s. He interviewed around 116,000 employees at IBM from 72 different countries. He derived four (later on expanded to five) cultural dimensions: power distance, individualism and collectivism, masculinity and femininity, uncertainty avoidance, and long-term and short-term orientation.

In collectivist cultures, the self is subjugated to the community. People in these cultures place others' interests before the self. This implies that decision making is by consensus and is a group rather than individual effort. The purpose is to avoid conflict and maintain harmony. People of collectivist cultures value

- group goals over individual goals;
- reciprocity in actions—granting of favors, for example;
- focus on personal disclosure to build rapport and trust;
- group consensus for decisions;
- face saving;
- group accomplishments over personal accomplishments;
- interdependence;
- family, loyalty, and personal ties.

Indians find it strange that in the United States and Great Britain, children of three months and above do not sleep with their parents but in their own rooms. In India, most children live with their parents, even after they get married, in a joint family system. Even in a nuclear family setup, close ties are maintained and usually, joint decisions are made.

In individualistic cultures, the self is prominent. Individuals are encouraged to have their personal goals and to make all efforts to achieve them. It is not expected that they be considerate of others (except family members). They are expected to make their own decisions. People of individualistic cultures value

- personal goals as distinct from group or family goals—emotional detachment from children and giving space and privacy to all;
- freedom and independence;
- personal time;
- personal accomplishment;
- competition with others.

Kenyan theology professor John S. Mbiti believes that the individual has little freedom to make choices without the consent of the family and the traditional community. He writes, "Whatever happens to the individual happens to the whole group, and whatever happens to the whole group happens to the individual. The individual can only say: 'I am, because we are; and since we are, therefore I am.' This is a cardinal point in the understanding of the African view of man.

Source: Lassiter (1999).

The VOM Approach

Kluckhohn and Strodtbeck (1961) presented a taxonomy of cultural values and proposed a Values Orientation Model theory (Hills 2002). According to them, every individual, regardless of culture, has to deal with five basic universal questions. Cultural anthropologists termed these as *value orientations* though essentially they are cultural patterns. The basic premise of this model is that humans share biological traits, which in turn gives birth to the concept of culture, and that people in general feel that their cultural traits and heritage are normal and even superior to those of others. Kluckhohn and Strodtbeck concluded that all people turn to their culture for assistance in responding to these value orientations.

The Kluckhohn and Strodtbeck model as illustrated in Table 2.1 shares several similarities with the Hofstede model in that each of the values move on a single continuum, and some of the characteristics are quite similar to the ones proposed by Hofstede.

Table 2.1 Description of five common human concerns with possible responses

Concerns/ orientations	Possible responses		
Human nature: What is the basic nature of people?	Evil: Most people can't be trusted. People are basically bad and need to be controlled.	Mixed: There are both evil people and good people in the world, and you have to check people out to determine which category they belong to. People can be changed with the right guidance.	Good: Most people are basically pretty good at heart; they are born good.
Man–nature relationship: What is the appropriate relationship with nature?	Subordinate to nature: People really can't change nature. Life is largely determined by external forces, such as fate and genetics. Whatever happens was meant to happen.	In harmony with nature: Man should, in every way, live in harmony with nature.	Dominant over nature: It is the great human challenge to conquer and control nature. Everything from air-conditioning to the green revolution has resulted from having met this challenge.
Time sense: How should we consider time?	Past: People should learn from history, draw the values they live by from history, and strive to continue past traditions into the future.	Present: The present moment is everything. Let's make the most of it. Don't worry about tomorrow; enjoy today.	Future: Planning and goal setting make it possible for people to accomplish miracles, to change and grow. A little sacrifice today will bring a better tomorrow.
Activity: What is the best mode of activity?	Being: It's enough to just be. It's not necessary to accomplish great things in life to feel your life has been worthwhile.	Becoming: The main purpose of being placed on this earth is for one's own inner development.	Doing: If people work hard and apply themselves fully, their efforts will be rewarded. What a person accomplishes is a measure of his or her worth.

Concerns/ orientations	Possible responses		
Social relations: What is the best form of social organization?	Hierarchical: There is a natural order to relations; some people are born to lead, and others are followers. Decisions should be made by those in charge.	Collateral: The best way to be organized is as a group, where everyone shares in the decision process. It is important not to make important decisions alone.	Individual: All people should have equal rights, and one should have complete control over one's own destiny. When we have to make a decision as a group, it should be: one person, one vote.

Source: Journal of Extension (n.d.).

Generalizations about the U.S. culture reveal the following traits:

- Is future oriented
- Focused on doing
- Emphasizes individualism
- Aspires to be dominant over nature
- Believes that human nature is mixed; some people are good and some are bad

In contrast, generalizations about traditional eastern cultures show the following traits:

- Is past oriented
- Focused on being
- Emphasizes collateral (group) relations
- Aspires to be in harmony with nature
- Believes that people are fundamentally good

The VOM theory recognizes that there are differences even within a culture. Responses could also change significantly with the degree of acculturation of the individual.

The Lewis Cross-Cultural Communication Model

In his book titled *When Cultures Collide*, Richard D. Lewis presented a model to classify cultures into three broad categories. His model facilitates greater understanding of the role of cultures in international negotiations, meetings, and presentations. The model was created to serve as a guide to interpret behavior of other cultures such as approach to time management, group or individualistic tendencies, direct or indirect communication preferences, power distance, and gender roles. It is useful in that it assists in a quick appraisal of one's own communication style in an intercultural context, in adapting to the requirements of other cultures, and in responding strategically to the challenges of the negotiation process.

The model (see Figure 2.1 in the following text) characterizes cultures into three groups: linear-active, multiactive, and reactive. The position of each culture is shown relative to other cultures in the form of a triangle.

For instance, if China wants to do business with France, this model would indicate to the Chinese that the following aspects are true concerning the French:

1. They are between highly linear-active and multiactive.
2. They are more formal and hierarchical than those from the United States.
3. Punctuality is moderately important.
4. They are somewhat talkative.
5. They tend to look at the big picture.
6. They value dialogue, debate, and discussions over consensus and groupthink.
7. They like details and inductive logic in their presentations.
8. They value relationships.

For the French, the model would help assess the cultural aspects of the Chinese such as:

1. They tend toward the reactive category.
2. They are the listening culture.

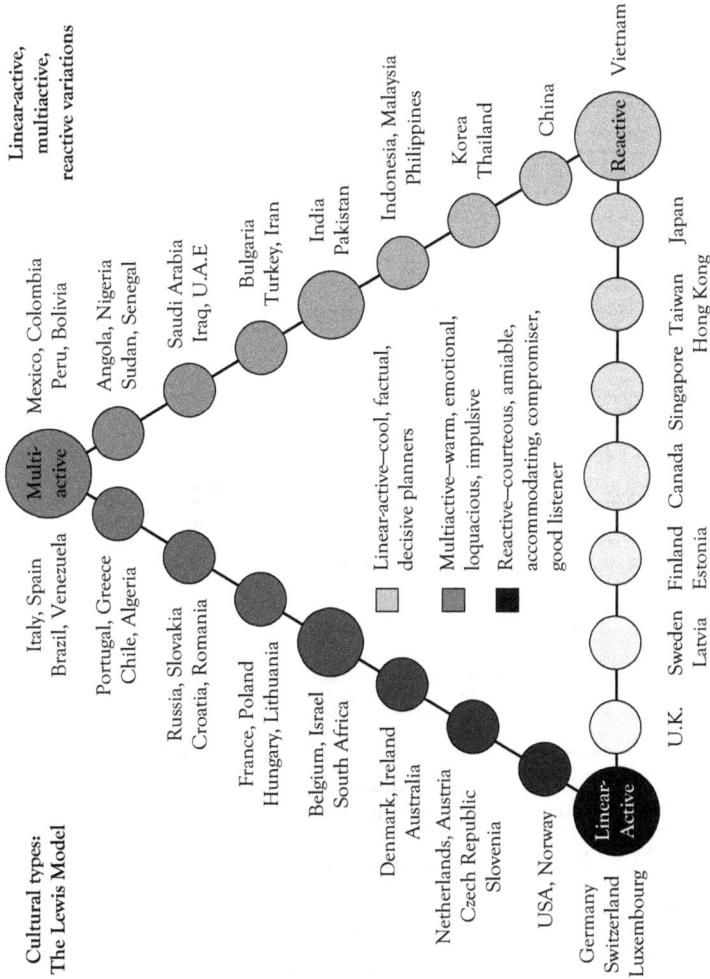

Figure 2.1 The Lewis model

3. They rely on data to make decisions.

4. They are very polite and indirect communicators.

5. Punctuality is valued with regard to time and deadlines.

6. They tend to hide their feelings.

7. Their facial expression is impassive.

8. They value relationships and believe in face saving of self and others (Table 2.2).

Table 2.2 Characteristic differences between the three styles in the Lewis model

Linear-active	Multiactive	Reactive
Talks less than the multiactives	Usually talkative	Usually listens
Obtains information and data from secondary sources	Obtains data and information from people	Uses both
Structured and well planned	Plans the big picture only	Focused on key areas only
Courteous and to the point	Emotional	Very courteous and indirect
Does not disclose feelings much	Displays emotions	Hides feelings and emotions
Confronts with logic	Confronts emotionally	Never confronts
Dislikes losing face	Has good excuses	Considers losing face as shameful
Breaks down tasks into parts and subparts	Tasks interplay and flow with one another	Looks at the whole picture
Rarely interrupts	Often interrupts	Doesn't interrupt
Task oriented	People oriented	Highly people oriented
Facts and evidence based	Juggles facts	Statements are promises
Truth before diplomacy	Flexible truth	Diplomacy over truth
Sometimes impatient	Impatient	Patient
Limited body language	Expansive body language	Subtle body language
Respects officialdom, position, and authority	Pulls strings to get work done	Networks extensively
Separates the personal and professional	Interweaves the personal and professional	Connects the social and professional
Does one thing at a time	Multitasks	Reacts to partner's action
Punctuality very important	Punctuality not that important	Punctuality important

The LESCANT Model

David Victor merged the concepts of Edward Hall's high-context and low-context cultures and created a continuum. On one end of the continuum were the explicit, direct communicators (Swiss, Germans, and Americans) and on the other end of the continuum were the implicit, indirect communicators such as Latin Americans, Arabs, and Japanese. The French and the British were placed in the middle of the continuum.

Victor closely links communication with culture. His LESCANT model offers a rich array of seven areas from which a cultural issue can arise when dealing with international business communication. The acronym LESCANT signifies the following:

L   **L**anguage: fluency, accents, and regional dialects and how they affect business communication; English as a global language

E   **E**nvironment: geography, population, topography, climate, food

S   **S**ocial organization: educational, political, and religious systems; class systems, role of women

C   **C**ontext: direct or indirect forms of communication; inductive and deductive reasoning

A   **A**uthority: attitude toward authority, leadership, and positional power; rule-observing or relationship-observing culture and how this impacts business communication; hierarchical and democratic power

N   **N**onverbal communication: movement, appearance, eye behavior, touching behavior, use of space and sound

T   **T**ime: how people divide time, schedule activities, and organize their day

Developing a Communication Strategy: A Model by Mary Munter

Distinguished author and communication expert Mary Munter designed a framework for developing a communication strategy in a global workplace (Reynolds and Valentine 2011). Munter added two more elements (medium and cultural context) to the existing communication model (comprising the communicator, message, the receiver, and feedback loop). A slightly modified version of the model is explained as follows with the help of an example.

Example: A Chinese business manager Chin Liu planned to import precision tools and specialized castings from Berlin, Germany. His purpose was to call the vendor, collect relevant information, and set a date to meet him. Which of the following actions would you advise him to take?

Step 1: Setting communication objectives

1. Place the call today.
2. Call after 6 p.m., after office hours.
3. Send an e-mail outlining your firm, introducing yourself, and the objective of your visit at least a week or two in advance of the requested appointment.
4. Tell your junior manager to call the manager in charge.
5. Send a request letter in German.
6. Avoid contacting during Easter time.

Correct strategy: Send an e-mail outlining your firm, introducing yourself, and the objective of your visit at least a week or two in advance; additionally, send a request letter in German; also avoid contacting during Easter time. Reason: Germans hate surprises. They are strictly monochromatic and value hierarchies. They cherish private time and treat work hours as being distinct from nonwork hours. Highly formal, they believe in strict protocol and seriousness in business dealings.

Step 2: Choosing a communication style

1. Play down your own title and position in the organization; after all, it's not good to boast in your culture.
2. Hire a translator to acquaint yourself with German meeting and negotiation styles.
3. Speak in English only—after all, that is the global language of business.
4. Prepare a detailed presentation down to the last bit of the proposal.
5. Let the discussion take its own course.

Correct strategy: Hire a translator to acquaint yourself with German meeting and negotiation styles. Prepare a detailed presentation down to the last bit of the proposal. Reason: Germans believe in power distance and are suitably impressed with credentials with a reasonable command of English. They are a fixed culture in that they value strict deadlines for everything. They have a penchant for detail and expect presentations with complete details.

Step 3: Assessing and enhancing credibility

1. Let your humility impress the German.
2. Discuss common values shared in business.
3. Focus on the achievements and the experience of the company.

Correct strategy: Focus on the achievements and the experience of the company. Reason: Germans are a rule-based culture and are impressed by credentials of the firm they are to deal with.

Step 4: Selecting and motivating your audience

1. Focus on personal relationship to influence.
2. Focus on rank and authority to influence.
3. Focus on material wealth to influence.
4. Focus on fair play to influence.
5. Focus on achievement and challenge to influence.

Correct strategy: Focus on rank and authority to influence; focus on achievement and challenge to influence. Reason: The influence strategy is dependent on the values upheld by the audience. In this case, Germans value achievement and fair play over wealth.

Step 5: Designing a message strategy for the first meeting

1. Write to the German to set an appointment.
2. Use a formal and a direct form of communication in an initial e-mail.

3. Ensure that follow-up messages such as e-mails and faxes are few and far between.
4. Ensure that follow-up messages are brief and to the point.

Correct strategy: Write to the German to set an appointment. Use a formal and direct form of communication in the first e-mail; follow-up messages should be brief and to the point.

Step 6: Overcoming language difficulties

1. Speak in English.
2. Have your business card printed in English as well as in German.
3. Avoid hiring translators as it would mount expenses.
4. Learn key words and phrases in German to get started.

Correct strategy: Have your business card printed in English as well as in German; you should learn key words and phrases in German to get started. Reason: Language should not be a barrier to communication; it's important to hire translators as the Germans are not well versed in English. The diction and the pronunciation is heavily emphasized.

Step 7: Using effective nonverbal behavior and prediscussion phase

1. Simply be natural.
2. Arrive on time (in fact before time).
3. Have a long handshake ceremony.
4. Compliment the hosts.
5. Use person's title and surname in greeting.
6. Lighten the environment by use of humor.
7. Be formal and polite.
8. Keep a large distance (personal space) between you and the vendor.
9. Dress informally.
10. Take red flowers as a gift.
11. Take lilies, carnations, and chrysanthemums as gifts.
12. Enter the meeting room quickly.

Correct strategy: Arrive on time (in fact before time). Use person's title and surname in greeting; be formal and polite. Reason: Germans are formal and do not appreciate humor at the beginning of an acquaintanceship. They value distance and keep work and nonwork time separate. Flowers are a no-no; red flowers indicate romantic interest.

Step 8: Discussion phase

1. List your achievements, lucidly highlighting what you can deliver.
2. Make numerous promises so that he is assured that you mean business.
3. Only talk facts.
4. Carry glitzy promotional material with you.
5. Expect bluntness and contradictions to your offerings and be prepared to deal with it.
6. Plan for a small talk just after the meeting with the key person.

Correct strategy: List achievements; talk facts; expect bluntness and contradictions and be prepared to deal with it. Reason: Germans do not indulge in small talk. They come straight to the point. Decision making is collaborative, although advice of the key person is taken.

Step 9: Negotiation stage

1. Quickly take a seat that should give you a vantage point.
2. Show the printed material, which is in English only.
3. Have a contract ready.
4. Be prepared for long-drawn-out rituals in the negotiation process.
5. Prepare contract in paragraphs.
6. Focus on pricing extensively.
7. Be prepared to argue, debate, and confront if necessary.
8. Pressure the Germans to accept the conditions offered by your firm.
9. Focus on facts, opinions, and emotions to influence the negotiation process.
10. Withhold some facts and bring them up later on.

Correct strategy: Be prepared for long-drawn-out rituals in the negotiation process; prepare contract in paragraphs; be prepared to argue, debate, and confront if necessary. Reason: Germans are a fixed culture and dislike surprises. They are vocal about their preferences and disagree forcefully. They rarely rely on emotions to persuade. Pricing and profits are not as big concerns to them as quality and precision.

Step 10: Others

1. Expect to be taken out for dinners and sightseeing.
2. Ask to be taken for a tour of their plant.
3. Phone the vendor at home to inquire casually about the status of the project.

Communication strategy: Ask to be taken for a tour of their plant. Reason: Unlike the Chinese who make extensive social engagements for their business visitors, Germans prefer to stick to the official routine. One is expected to make one's own sightseeing arrangements. At the most, a request for a tour of the plant may be acceded to.

Intercultural Communication Continuum

Most of the continuum was more culture oriented than communication oriented in approach. I created a continuum based on communication variables that impact international business. This was on the lines of the work done by previous authors in the field.

Description of the Model

The model comprised nine communication variables that had the potential to impact communication in international interactions. These included the following:

1. Task orientation versus relationship orientation
2. Conflict friendly versus conflict averse
3. Low level of disclosure versus high level of disclosure

4. Reliance on cognitive knowledge versus reliance on affective knowledge
5. Linear speech pattern versus circular speech pattern
6. Horizontal versus vertical lines of communication
7. Voluble body language versus reserved body language
8. Preference for high level of team communication versus preference for individualistic style of communication
9. Preference for deductive and informal written style of correspondence versus preference for formal and inductive style of written correspondence

I tested the model in my intercultural classroom. Students were given different-colored beads signifying the nine communication variables. Groups of 13 students were assigned a country and taking the help of the Lewis model were required to plot the communication preference of that country across the nine variables. One bead was required to be pasted on the continuum sheet given to them. In this manner, a beautiful necklace was created for that particular country. There were three such groups and consequently three countries, each with a unique communication necklace.

The scores for each country were then plotted on a master sheet, which had all the three countries in perspective (see Appendix A at the end of this chapter). Students could visualize the communication distance between each country and could plan their responses better.

Summary

1. A cultural deglobalization has taken place due to the increasing internationalization of business. More than ever before, people are now anxious to preserve their cultural roots and resist cultural imperialism.
2. Cultural anthropologists, sociologists, and psychologists have created several models and frameworks based on their extensive study of diverse cultures.
3. Cultural models and frameworks are important as these help to compare the similarities and differences among two or more cultures on certain international variables.

4. Edward Hall introduced the concept of contexting in communication and divided people into two categories of communicators—the low-context and the high-context communicators. He also introduced the concept of monochromic and polychromic cultures.

5. Hofstede introduced four (later on expanded to five) cultural dimensions—power distance, individualism and collectivism, masculinity and femininity, uncertainty avoidance, and long-term and short-term orientation—when he consulted for IBM.

6. Kluckhohn and Strodtbeck (1961) presented a taxonomy of cultural values and proposed a VOM theory. According to them, every individual, regardless of culture, has to deal with five basic universal questions. Kluckhohn and Strodtbeck concluded that all people turn to their culture for assistance in responding to these value orientations.

7. Richard D. Lewis presented a model to classify cultures into three broad categories—linear-active, multiactive and reactive. This was to facilitate better understanding of the role of cultures in international negotiations, meetings, and presentations.

8. Victor closely links communication with culture. His LESCANT model offers a rich array of variables—seven areas in which a cultural issue can arise when dealing with international business communication.

9. Mary Munter's framework for communication strategy includes two important components—cultural context and medium, in addition to the existing communication model (comprising the communicator, message, the receiver, and feedback loop). This model serves as the ultimate guideline to plan a communication strategy for a cross-cultural event.

10. An intercultural communication continuum was created to understand the communication distance between cultures.

Key Terms

- Cultural deglobalization
- Cultural imperialism
- Cultural pluralism
- Iceberg effect
- Contexting

- Cultural values
- Intercultural communication continuum

Appendix A: Classroom Activity on Intercultural Communication Modeling

Intercultural communication continuum
Countries : USA (——) China (······) and France (- - -)

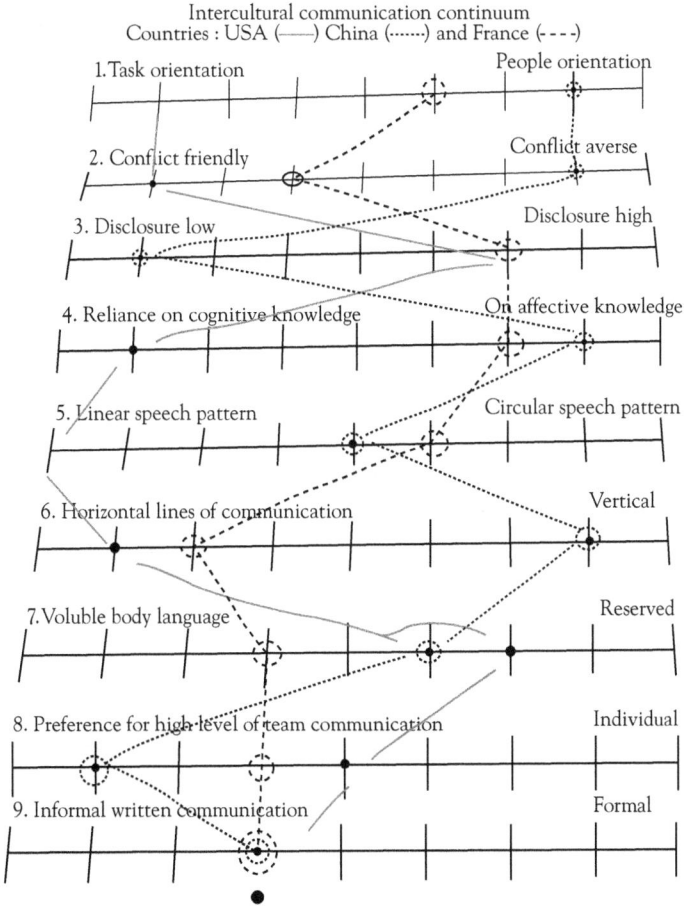

1. Task orientation — People orientation
2. Conflict friendly — Conflict averse
3. Disclosure low — Disclosure high
4. Reliance on cognitive knowledge — On affective knowledge
5. Linear speech pattern — Circular speech pattern
6. Horizontal lines of communication — Vertical
7. Voluble body language — Reserved
8. Preference for high level of team communication — Individual
9. Informal written communication — Formal

CHAPTER 3

Language and Communication

"You should say what you mean," the March Hare told Alice in Alice in Wonderland. "I do," Alice replied, "at least I mean what I say— that's the same thing, you know." "Not the same thing a bit!" said the Hatter, "You might as well say that 'I see what I eat' is the same thing as 'I eat what I see"
—Lewis Carol, Alice's Adventures in Wonderland, 1865

Introduction

Communication is the creative force that drives processes in organizations. Manifesting in dialogue, rhetoric, speech acts, and nonverbal expressions, communication processes drive, evolve, change, and unify organizations. Far from being merely a functional division in organizations, communication has now become a powerful enabler for the growth, development, and consolidation of organizations.

Communicative Competence

The essence of communicative competence is that language and culture are inseparable in expressing one's point of view. Linguistic knowledge includes grammar and the rules that govern discourse. Sociocultural knowledge involves the choices people make on the basis of their contextual background. Communication is integral to an organization, with various situations demanding different forms of communication that are culturally defined (Figure 3.1).

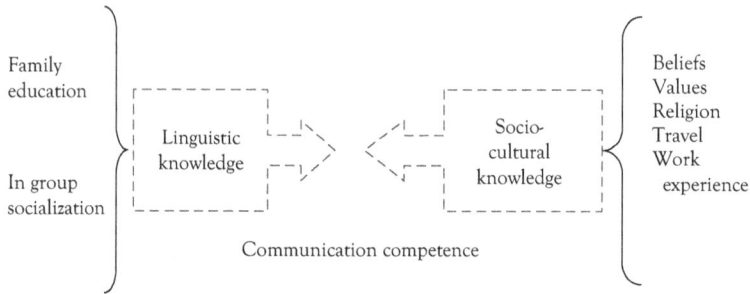

Figure 3.1 Antecedents of communication competence

Language and Communication

Though technology has fueled globalization, technology alone cannot achieve globalization. The important role played by language as a sharing facility and an enabler of communication between individuals and companies (and countries) to communicate cannot be understated. Language itself is an evolved cultural pattern.

More international business is done between nonnative English speakers than between native English speakers. In 2005, *Newsweek International* published an article on the rise of English around the world. Quoting English language expert David Crystal (1997), the article reports that nonnative speakers of English now outnumber native speakers 3 to 1. There are more Chinese children studying English— about 100 million—than there are Britons. It concluded then that within a decade (by 2015), 2 billion people would be studying English and about half the world—some 3 billion people—would be speaking it.

As cross-cultural exchanges happen in a connected world, language remains in focus. It is important to take into account, however, that the pragmatic purposes of English in international business do not typically call for the same breadth of lexicon and grammar as some of the other activities. In fact, native speakers often need as much help as nonnatives when using English to interact internationally.

Research suggests that the English Lingua Franca (ELF) communication seems "too partial a view for globalized business." Failure to communicate in the language of the new country may result in pragmatic failure—the inability to understand what is meant by what is said. Pragmatic failure results in the misinterpretation of the utterances, the way the speaker intends them. This leads to frustration and cross-cultural communication breakdowns. The rise of Hinglish, Chinglish, and Spanglish is a positive step to reduce the linguistic ethnocentricity that had engulfed the world till sometime back.

Media attention has now focused on a new phonetic writing system developed by an investment banker George Jabbour to assist new language learners read, understand, and speak their target language. A Syrian visiting England for higher studies, Jabbour had trouble pronouncing English words, which created stark barriers between the locals and foreigners. The new system, called *SaypU*, an acronym for *Spell As You Pronounce Universally*, can be applied to all languages; visitors to foreign countries would be able to read signs, maps, labels, and menus without learning a new writing system.

Source: Meritt (2013).

According to Charles (2007), in the environment of global diversity, it is Business English Lingua Franca (BELF), and not ELF, that is going to pave the way for effective conduct of international business. The BELF approach differs from ELF in that the domain of the former is only business and its frame of reference is the globalized business community. "Whatever language becomes the lingua franca of global business, faster and more accurate translation services and products are needed" (Zipperer 2001).

Katakana eigo

In the Japanese language, consonants such as *v* are nonexistent. Consonants are always attached to the vowels and never used distinctly. This results in *katakana eigo* or English interpretation produced by joining the building blocks of the Japanese alphabet. Thus, first and fast may sound the same (fa-su-to) when spoken by the Japanese.

Source: c JETRO (1999).

Studies indicate that the Internet use of Mandarin, Hindi, and Spanish is rising. Graddol (1997) cautions that if regional trading blocs increase in number and in influence, English could become irrelevant within some of the blocs. Similarly, if translation software improves, businesspeople might stop needing a common language altogether.

When speaking English, the Japanese tend to confuse by and until. If the speaker says, "I will be in India until August 15" and actually meant that he would be reaching India by August 15, then serious communication errors may arise.

Charles (2007) described three responses companies can take to address language issues:

- Techno-oriented companies address the language issue by installing sophisticated language software or hiring translators.
- Rule-bound companies address the issue by standardizing the spoken and written communication language.
- Forward-looking companies address the language issue by enabling and facilitating the understanding of different cultures and the way of speaking. They do this by heightening the awareness of communicative and cultural diversity and increasing the English used globally.

The Rise of Indian English: The International Language of Globalization

"Prepaid mobile phones have become so ubiquitous in India that English words to do with their use—recharge, top-up and missed call—have become common, too. Now, it seems, those words are transforming to take on broader meanings in Indian languages as well as in Hinglish" (Lahiri 2012).

In 2005, a new edition of the *Collins English Dictionary* included 26 neologisms of Indian origin. In a statement, the dictionary has officially acknowledged the role of Hinglish in the evolution of

English. The *Concise Oxford Dictionary* the world's most credible collection of words has turned eclectic, incorporating several Indianisms. Many words of daily use in English are of Indian origin, including words such as shampoo, bangle, bungalow, jungle, mantra, pundit, and cot. Even though purists are agitated about it, the *Oxford Dictionary* has acknowledged "a public demonstration" as the meaning of "agitation," which is more in use in India and is vastly different from the traditional English usage as "irregular motion or disturbance."

According to a statement by Collins, "the inclusion of Hinglish words in the Dictionary marks an exciting development and a new phase of borrowing by English." Hinglish, it appears, is playing a greater role in the business world. According to the article, advertising has "started shifting from pure Hindi or English advertisements to Hindi with a few words of English thrown in." Multinational companies such as Domino's Pizza, Pepsi, and Coca Cola are using Hinglish to appeal to local sensitivities. Thus the Pepsi slogans include "Yeh dil maange more" ("Ask for more") and 'Bas abhi ke abhi' ("Want things right now"), while Coke relies on "Life ho to aisi" ("Life should be like this") and Dominos Pizza on 'Hungry Kya?' ("Are you hungry?").

Language and Speech Acts

People belonging to different groups, subgroups, and communities have different ways of using language to communicate, and their ways of using speech define them as a group, subgroup, culture, and community. Thus, no two groups or communities have the same communicative competencies. The situation is compounded in a cross-cultural context because groups are defined or limited by their respective communicative competencies. For example, in comparison to the Danes, the French use verbs in an abstract manner; their nouns are also changed to verbs, imparting a rather abstract character to the French language. The French language uses a hierarchical structure in text and communication such that the information in sentences is often organized in subordinate structures (for example, by nonfinite verb forms). The Danish language uses a linear structure for presenting and organizing information in coordinate sentences, which have as their center, verbs in the finite form of past, present, or future (Lundquist 2009).

Deborah Tannen (1984) describes three broad levels of differences, which can create misunderstanding in a cross-cultural interaction:

- When to say
- What to say
- How to say, which includes pacing and pausing, listening, intonation and prosody, formulaicity, indirectness, and cohesion and coherence

The potential areas for misunderstanding are elaborated upon in the sections that follow (level 3 has been dealt with more elaborately in the next chapter).

When to Say

When to say represents the most general level of communication that is relative to the culture. For instance, most East Asian cultures such as Japan, China, Taiwan, Thailand, Singapore, Korea, and a few African cultures such as Swaziland, Ethiopia, and Kenya value silence. In these cultures, when *not* to talk is a more appropriate question than when to talk. Silence in these cultures is also a form of communication. The Japanese word *haragei*, the Korean term *noon-chi*, and the Chinese term *mo-chi* indicate the value attributed to silence by the East Asian societies. Among Westerners, the Swedes and the Finns are more reticent than the French and Germans. Americans, the British, and Australians are referred to as the *talkative* cultures.

For many Easterners, silence does not indicate disinterest, inaction, or a failure to communicate as is commonly perceived in some Western societies (see Table 3.1 in the following text). Silence can communicate the following:

- The person is contemplating a response to a question
- The person is agreeing to what the other person is saying
- The person is expressing dissent

Table 3.1 Silence and its interpretation in diverse cultures

S. no.	Silence as perceived by East Asian cultures	Silence as perceived by European, American, and Australian cultures
1	Speech regarded as distraction to the thinking process; silence allows contemplation	Speech associated with expression and clarity of thought; silence regarded as uncomfortable break in conversation
2	Silence associated with wisdom; allows people to plan	Silence leads to awkwardness between the parties, especially when it is too long
3	Silence gives people time to collect thoughts before responding	Silence leads to view such people as unsocial and uncooperative
4	Silence helps people to interpret the speaker correctly	Silence creates ambiguity
5	Silence allows the speaker opportunity to rephrase the question	Silence results in waste of time and resources
6	Silence saves the face of the speaker especially when the receiver disagrees	Silence delays action; depicts apathy of the listeners
7	Silence saves the face of self, especially observed in persons with low level of English language fluency	Silence creates unwarranted judgments about competency and confidence
8	Silence is associated with power	Silence is deemed manipulative

Source: Nakane (2007).

- The person is angry
- The person is anxious and suffers from communication apprehension
- The person is waiting for the seniors to speak up first

Silence and its occurrence cannot be examined in isolation. Its basis lies in physical, psychological, linguistic, stylistic, and interactive factors. Experts also suggest that cultures can be mapped on a continuum from the most verbal to the most silent.

What to Say

Once a decision has been made to talk, the next logical question is what to say. This includes the following speech acts: questions, agreement and disagreement, asking for information, humor and irony, opinions, compliments, apologies, and advice.

Questions

Socrates defined teaching as the *art of asking questions*. Asking questions is considered important to aid in the construction of meaning and to make sense of the information presented. It facilitates knowledge creation and dissemination. Questioning serves many useful purposes. It allows for reflection and internalization of the concepts, it is a form of feedback to the speaker, and it paves the way for greater interactivity and participation in the classroom. In most classrooms, questioning takes up almost a third of the teaching time.

Questioning is widely used in many corporate boardrooms. Google, a well-known tech company, prides itself on the culture of questioning that it has created in the organization.

Questioning is also deeply rooted in the psyche of the culture to which the person belongs. In societies that have a large power distance, there is great distance between the parents and the children, the teacher and the taught, the boss and the subordinate, and the government officials and the common person. Respect and obedience to the elders and those in power is expected, and any deviation from the same can be perceived as threatening (Hofstede et al. 2010). With respect to the education sector, teachers inspire awe and fear. Usually teaching is teacher centered with emphasis on rote rather than learning. Japan, China, South Korea, Singapore, India, and Mexico are examples of cultures that have a high power distance.

In my class on intercultural communication, I observed that among the Europeans, the French asked the most questions, while the Swiss asked the least questions. Not surprisingly, the native Indian students asked the least number of questions in accordance with their cultural norms of deference.

In Korea, the teacher is revered like a king. Taiwanese students do not question the content or the teaching process at all out of respect for the teacher. In fact, many students in Taiwan prefer teacher-centered authority despite educational reviews calling for more student-centered learning. In Japan, students would rather ask other students than the teacher for clarifications, if any. Similarly, in Mexico and India, questions from students are highly improbable (even in higher education); the instruction style is lecture driven and teacher centered. In China, two broad strategies are common for eliciting responses—the hint strategy and the query strategy. Examples could be, "I feel that we should not go ahead with the project" (the aim was to know what the recipient felt). The query strategy is more direct, such as, "Do you have any suggestions?" or "What do you think of the proposal?"

Expressing Disagreement

The *Oxford Dictionary* defines disagree as *to have or express a different opinion.* It may also imply attacking the position held by another person or silently conveying displeasure. In an American culture, it is considered a virtue to be assertive and expressive about one's views and opinions (Samovar and Porter 2001). In contrast, in the Japanese culture, it is important to avoid conflicts and maintain harmony; voicing one's opinion is a measured strategy rather than an impulsive one. Though Hofstede (1997) claimed that collectivist cultures were more indirect in saying no or refusing requests, studies report that cultures such as Korea and China are more direct than even the most individualistic cultures (Australia, for example, or even Great Britain). In a study of rhetoric in an actual business meeting, Yeung reported that the Chinese delegates asked more questions and made more requests than Australians, that Australians hedged more (using words like perhaps; I think that; Yes, but...), and that most Chinese delegates used more negative words to start their sentences (but, no) than the Australians.

> Chinese rule for disagreement: It's more important to give constructive suggestions than to show respect for the higher status of others. Australians preface their disagreements with "Yes, but..."
> *Source:* Spencer-Oatey (2000).

Some cultures tend to use mitigation devices to avoid direct confrontation. Fiona Johnson (2006) lists a following few:

Hedging   This is a strategy used to understate the illocutionary point of the utterance. The speaker avoids making a firm commitment. The words used are kind of, maybe, and I think so are used frequently by the Japanese to avoid a direct clash of ideas (Kobayashi and Viswat 2010). In India, if one has to disagree or decline an invitation, it is normal to use the euphemism: I'll think about it.

Downtoners   In this strategy, the tone or the vocal impact is sought to be reduced by modulating the impact of the utterance. Words used are probably, may, and perhaps.

Hesitators   In this strategy, the speaker deliberately hesitates to reveal qualms about the veracity of the idea proposed by another. Words used are err or umm.

Appealers   This strategy aims to appease the hearer directly so that a positive response is elicited from the hearer. Phrases include I agree with you, but…You may be right, but…You see….

Another category, the **reasoners** can be added. They try to reason out their viewpoint without appearing to be offensive. Phrases include the following: The way I see it. . . I'm against it because. . . Instead, I think that. . . I'm afraid I don't agree with you, because… The British often use this technique to disagree politely.

Yet another way to disagree in some culture is to offer solutions. These are the **solvers** and they use phrases such as I think we should. . . We could. . . One solution may be. . . .

Telling people how you feel about something requires a bit of finesse in some cultures. You have to be able to say what you want to say without offending the other person. For the British, this often means finding roundabout ways of saying what you want to say and using a lot of polite expressions in your speech. Frankness is something that English speakers do not necessarily appreciate.

Source: Norman (n.d.).

Expressing Agreement

The simplest way to acknowledge an agreement is to nod one's head. Phrases include "Hmmm," "That's a good idea," "I think you are right," and "I completely agree with you." In Japan however, head nods are not to be interpreted literally (more on head nods in the next chapter). Their ways of expressing agreement are also rather ambivalent; agreement is more about the person, not the premise. Due to the collectivist orientation, Japanese differentiate between *honne* (their true feelings or opinions) and *tatamae* (the appropriate thing to say in a situation). This is a cause of deep-rooted frustration for non-Japanese businesspeople as they are not able to make a distinction between what constitutes *honne* and what constitutes *tatamae*. The Japanese yes can mean anything from "I am understanding you," "I am listening to you," and "I am listening to you even if I do not agree with what you say," to "Please continue with what you are saying."

In India, when a host inquires, "Would you like to have a cold drink?" it is almost customary to refuse the first time. The conversation would continue something like this: "No, I am quite full." This will prompt the host to say, "Oh! You hardly ate anything! A cold drink would do no harm." The guest would reply: "Well…alright. Just give me in a small glass." Indeed the guest would be quite taken aback if the host did not ask him or her again!

Requests for Information

People belonging to high-context collectivist cultures typically require a lot of information to assist them in decision making. This is distinct from the low-context countries, which focus on the information that they need to know to complete the task assigned to them. For most Americans time is money, and they would rather not spend time on unnecessary information that does not add value. However, if a Japanese requires X information, it will be implicit that he or she would also like to have information Y and Z to successfully complete a task. Requests therefore in the Japanese culture are not explicit and clear; they merely indicate the starting point from which more such requests could follow. The requests are therefore characterized as vague, in piecemeal format, and requiring frequent follow-up by foreigners dealing with the Japanese.

In China, the situation is vastly different even if the country possesses somewhat similar cultural traits as the Japanese. The Chinese (as well as those from Taiwan and Korea) prefer to be direct in expressing requests for information and abstain from beating around the bush. Like the Japanese, a vast majority of Indians are indirect communicators and come to the point later on in the conversation especially when a relationship has not been established with the information seeker.

Humor and Irony

What results in laughter is not universal; it is dependent on many sociocultural variables. Humor may not always result in laughter and is not always regarded as amusing. Cultures have different interpretations of what constitutes humor. For the French, humor is more a play on words. Irony is characteristic of Danish humor. Indians cannot appreciate laughing at themselves, while they openly laugh at others' misfortunes.

Cultures also vary in their preference for topics of humor. Blonde jokes are common in the United States. Similarly, other cultures have a preference for jokes on mothers-in-law, wives, politics, and religion. In Japan, humor is governed by conventions such as those relating to harmony, cooperation, formality, and membership of an in-group. Humor in Japan is rarely spontaneous and impulsive. American humor tends to be rather over the top and exaggerated and ignores conventions of formality and hierarchy. A typical American sarcasm would be followed by "Just kiddin'." British humor tends to be dry and witty (often the Oscar Wilde variety), whereas Canadian humor is satirical in nature. Canadians tend to provoke people by making fun of them, and there have been instances in which Canada has been rebuked for political incorrectness. A well-known instance is that of the Canadian Prime Minister Pierre Trudeau (known for his unconventional ways) who was caught by photographer Doug Ball spinning a pirouette behind an oblivious Queen Elizabeth during a G7 Summit conference in the Buckingham Palace, London, England, on May 7, 1977. "The picture expresses his maverick anti-conformism, his democratic disdain for aristocratic pomp," noted Ball.

Irreverent body language?: Trudeau in focus

Source: Trudeau (1977).

In some countries such as Denmark and Belgium, people deliberately make light of topics that make people anxious, such as those related to death, old age, loneliness, and illness.

Complimenting

The convention of paying and receiving compliments differs across cultural boundaries. Praise and compliments play an important role in communication. Compliments fall into two major categories: those having to do with appearance (for a person as well as objects) and those having to do with ability (of the person or the specific act of ability). Wolfson (1983) regards rapport building as the primary function of compliments. She also indicates that expressions of gratitude, greeting, conversation starters, or leave taking are also different functions of compliments.

The functions of praise could be any one of the following:

- To encourage others: Teachers in any society would like to encourage young children with phrases such as "You can really draw well" or "That's a great piece of writing; well done and keep it up!"

- To build relationships: Praise is meant to make receivers feel good about themselves and is also about the person who is complimenting. Phrases include "That was a sumptuous feast!," or "You are so efficient!"
- To create an atmosphere of goodwill: This type of praise is given initially at the start of an important conversation so that the receiver(s) are appeased before any bad news or negative feedback is given. Thus instead of a greeting, the conversation would start with a praise or a compliment. Phrases include "Wow! Looking good!"; "Nice tie."

Research by Li Feilin and Yu Gaofeng (2005) reveals interesting differences between the complimenting styles of the British, the Americans, and the Chinese. They observe that in the English language, people prefix the personal pronoun "I" before complimenting someone, such as "I love your dress!" The Chinese however use the second person to prefix the compliment in English language, for example, "You do this work really nicely!" Americans regard praise or compliments with respect to a person's ability a serious matter; hence only a qualified person can compliment somebody's achievement. This is not so with Chinese where usually a junior compliments the senior (rather than vice versa) so as to make an impression on him.

In some cultures, it is almost customary to disagree with a compliment. In India for example, if someone says, "This dress looks good on you," it is expected that the receiver would respond with something like this: "Oh, this? This is quite old! I purchased this in Delhi five years ago!" Even the Chinese respond with a disagreement to a compliment. They add a question and also a fault to the object of the compliment. "You like this watch? (question) Why, it's quite old and has at least two scratches!" (fault). On the contrary, Japanese do not feel the need to pay a personal compliment to their wives or children. Their compliments, when paid to others, are tempered with humility. For example, they may say, "Your country is so green and beautiful. In comparison my country looks like a marooned, dry island!" This kind of humility makes the recipient feel that the Japanese compliment is insincere and that the speaker is hoping that the recipient will use a disclaimer to counter the assertion, such as "No, no, even your country is very beautiful!"

Some cultures exaggerate when they compliment. For example, the British use hyperbole extensively to praise others. Arabs have a unique way of complimenting. Known for reciting couplets, proverbs, and poetry, they compliment using eloquent words and use metaphors, analogies, and imagery. Compliments are woven into the fabric of the Arab way of life. Complimenting is a way to appease, to flatter, and to indulge another mainly to serve self-interest. Arabs focus more on the eloquent delivery of the compliment than the compliment itself.

> When they enter a shop, Arabs might say something to this effect: "We have visited your shop because we understand that you are the best...give us a hefty discount and we will bring more customers to your shop."

Giving and Receiving Advice

Cultural nuances are also observed in the speech act of giving and receiving advice. When people make decisions, they usually seek advice from others. However, some advice is unsolicited and has the adverse effect of threatening the autonomy of the recipient. Unsolicited advice from relatives, friends, and strangers may appear inappropriate in cultural contexts when it is viewed as potentially intrusive and condescending to the recipient, as if to convey that the recipient lacks knowledge or the competency to make choices independently.

Collectivist cultures are known to be more tolerant of advice than individualistic cultures. In the United States and Western Europe, advice from relatives, friends, and strangers is seen as highly intrusive and that which fosters unnecessary relational interdependence. This is in contrast to Russia where almost anybody and everybody can give advice (Chentsova-Dutton and Vaughn 2011). In India, one is supposed to seek advice (even one is not in need of it) so as to give importance to a close relative, patriarchs in the family, bosses, and superiors. The central idea in this culture is to ensure that the decision has been made with the consent of all.

I am a Dutch living in the UK and I totally agree that they (the British) are very closed on this subject (of giving and receiving advice). Whenever I am back in the Netherlands people in the shop talk to me or warn me when my kids are in trouble. In the UK it is just a big silence. (This) does not make me feel welcome. Even at work people don't really tell the way they see it. Which makes me feel lonely some-time. However this is how it is in the South of England. I also come in the North of England and people are their more curious and ask more. Which is nice (*sic*).

Source: Meghan Fenn (2012).

Languages are used in two contexts—the language of ordinary, everyday conversation and the language of business. The language of business is the language of trade. The trade language can be the English language or its hybrid versions, or, a regional trade language such as Persian or Chinese. Either way, language should serve as the common ground that facilitates rather than hinders business. Translation services, interlocutors, and interpreters can be utilized to improve the quality and clarity of busi-ness conversations.

Summary

1. Communication has now become a powerful enabler for the growth, development, and consolidation of organizations.
2. The essence of communicative competence is that language and cul-ture are inseparable. Both linguistic as well as sociocultural knowl-edge is important for effectively expressing putting one's point of view.
3. Language itself is an evolved cultural pattern. Currently, the debate is that ELF communication seems too partial a view for globalized business and that it must be substituted by BELF.
4. Failure to communicate in the language of the new country may result in pragmatic failure—the inability to understand what is

meant by what is said. If regional trading blocs increase in number and in influence, English could become irrelevant within some of the blocs.

5. Three broad levels of differences, which can create misunderstandings in a cross-cultural interaction are (1) when to say, (2) what to say, and (3) how to say (dealt with more elaborately in the next chapter).

Key Terms

- Communicative competence
- ELF and BELF
- Pragmatic failure
- Silence
- Speech acts

CHAPTER 4

Nonverbal Messages

Fie, fie upon her! There's language in her eye, her cheek, her lip, Nay, her foot speaks; her wanton spirits look out at every joint and motive of her body.

—Ulysses in William Shakespeare's Troilus and
Cressida, IV.5.54-57

Introduction

From the time Charles Darwin published his epoch study—*Expressions of the Emotions in Man and Animals* in 1872, researchers from diverse disciplines such as anthropology, sociology, and, now, management, have been interested in exploring body language and its interpretation in various cultures. Nonverbal communication is an outward reflection of a person's emotional condition. More than verbal communication, it is the nonverbal communication that reveals the true attitudes and emotions of people, often without their conscious awareness. People both consciously and subconsciously tend to reveal their likes and dislikes through their body language.

Nonverbal communication is a product of culture and tends to be interpreted in a culture-specific way. People from native cultures speak their own language and follow particular cultural norms. In a multicultural workplace, negative micromessages may be sent to members of minority or ethnic groups (people who are perceived to be different from the majority), even if their verbal messages are polite and courteous. Negative micromessages can include a sneer, a cynical smile, raised eyebrows, a casual shrug, a smug facial expression, and the like. This subtle form of communication complicates relationships and provides a subconscious source of misunderstandings across cultures. It also has the potential to affect performance and output.

Randhir Garg, an Indian, working as a guest worker in Great Britain, is regarded by fellow British employees as nonassertive and lazy. Though they do not say anything to him verbally, they send him micromessages conveying a negative stereotype. Garg feels like an outsider, thus affecting his performance in the team.

Nonverbal communication includes all forms of communication excluding the language used to speak or write. Three types of nonverbal communication will be discussed in this text: body language (facial expressions, gestures, posture, and body movements); physical environment (using physical space, distance and proximity norms, and territorial control); and personal attributes (such as appearance, voice, and touch). Technically, the study of body language is termed as kinesics, oculesics, proxemics, haptics, vocalics, chronemics, and environment.

Nonverbal communication is very important in international business, partly because verbal communication can be (more often than not) misleading or unreliable. This is especially true in international business negotiations, cross-country presentations, international product launches, as well as all communication related to mergers and acquisitions. International marketing often relies on the nonverbal communication of target population participants in focus group discussions for brand decisions.

Types of Nonverbal Communication

Nonverbal communication can be classified into two categories: conscious messages and subliminal messages. Senders of conscious messages are aware that they are sending out a particular message and that the message has a definite implication. For example, a thumbs-up signal by an American is positive, denoting good job or go ahead. Receivers of the conscious nonverbal message know that the message is a positive one and a sign of motivation. In contrast, subliminal messages appeal to the subconscious mind of the receiver. A receiver is not consciously aware of the nonverbal message. Organizations that require its employees to wear uniforms subliminally communicate position, authority, and a desire for belongingness among those wearing them. The advertising media also uses subliminal messages. For example, in a movie, an actor is seen drinking cola of a reputed company. The use of these products in the movie would not be classified strictly as advertisements. However, the mere association of the movie with the brand and the product transmits subliminal messages that influence the viewers.

Nonverbal messages can be involuntary as well as voluntary. People unintentionally convey many messages through their facial expressions, hand movements, and eye contact. It is often said that liars can be caught merely by telltale signals: shifty eyes, gestures of touching nose and ear, and even by the way they smile. Because involuntary communication is unplanned, it represents a better assessment of people's true intentions than verbal messages. Nonverbal communication can also be voluntary. People knowledgeable about body language can control their nonverbal responses. They take special care to avoid the telltale signs that may reveal their true intent.

Functions of Nonverbal Communication

Mindful nonverbal communication has the following distinct functions:

Enhancing, Asserting, and Reflecting Identities

Nonverbal cues serve as identity badges. We tend to respond to others on the basis of stereotypes rather than personal content characteristics. The face, hair, eyes, clothes, and accessories are interpreted by others through the medium of stereotypes. Accent, posture, and gesture also reveal group membership (Asian? American? Japanese?). Categorical slotting takes place as a result of speech patterns, physical cues (such as hair and skin color), and clothing. Vocalics such as speech, accent, pitch intensity, volume, and articulation also characterize cultural origins. We tend to like people who sound like us in contrast to those who sound very different.

Expressing Emotions

Feelings and attitudes are inferred from kinesics and vocalics. The human face is said to be capable of producing 2,50,000 facial expressions. Culture shapes emotional expressions. Subconsciously, through the cultural reinforcement process, people internalize the nonverbal rules of their culture. They react spontaneously to situations through learned behavior. It is thus that human beings acquire nonverbal display rules. They learn when to suppress emotions and how and when to convey emotions. Thus, collectivists will learn to suppress display (to maintain relationships and preserve harmony), while the individualists will learn to express display of emotions, feelings, and behavior.

Though members of various cultures universally acknowledge happiness and surprise, feelings of disgust, anger, unhappiness, or hurt are more obviously demonstrated by the expressive cultures better than the reserved cultures. Additionally, the smile can be interpreted in different ways. While in the United States the smile is an expression of joy, in Japan, it may imply a myriad of emotions (including embarrassment, displeasure, or anger). Russians, for example, rarely smile at the beginning of a negotiation, but as it progresses in a favorable manner, they start to smile. In terms of vocalics, the Arabs, Italians, and Greeks tend to raise their voices and argue passionately; while they are not angry, to an American they might appear to be so. From an Arab's point of view, the American tone may sound cold, distant, and aloof, but to an Asian it may sound too aggressive and harsh. Thus, cultural relativism can impact how people perceive each other.

Meaning of a smile in various cultures	
United States:	Friendliness
Asia:	Friendliness, covering for emotional pain, embarrassment, anger
Russia:	Agreement, satisfaction

Managing Conversations

People use kinesics and oculesics (eye contact) to manage their conversations with each other. Kinesics includes emblems, illustrators, regulators, and adaptors, and each of these has a specific communication objective. They are not, however, mutually exclusive. An emblem is an intentional hand gestures that has a specific meaning attributed to it. Consider the *ok* sign, for example. The use of this signal means good in the United States, money in Japan, a sexual insult in Greece, zero in French, and vulgar in Russia. The thumbs-up gesture means good or great in the United States and Great Britain, but is offensive to Arabs. The use of gestures may lead to misunderstandings, as a polite greeting in one culture may be considered rude in another culture.

Meaning of hand gestures in various cultures

Italy	In counting, thumb means one and index finger means two
Australia	Index finger is one and middle finger is two
United States	*V* is for victory with outward palm
Great Britain	*V* is for victory when the palm faces the receiver; it is an insult when palm faces the speaker (same for Australia, New Zealand)
Japan, Korea, Taiwan	*V* with outward palm (facing the receiver), especially when photographed
Philippines	*V* is for peace
Vietnam	*V* is for hello
Indonesia	Index finger is used to stop public transport
United States	People are beckoned with palm up
Korea	People are beckoned by snapping fingers
Europe	Thumbs-up gesture means one
Greece	Thumbs-up means "one up to you"
United States	Handshake to greet
Japan	Bow to greet (depth of the bow indicates respect for seniority and position)

Illustrators are hand gestures that complement the spoken words. These gestures help to visualize the imagery and are the most pictorial of the nonverbal gestures. These are mostly used to illustrate directions. The Italians, Greeks, and Spaniards use more illustrators than the Americans. Arabs, South Americans, and Egyptians use animated illustrators.

Belgians, Finns, and those from Asian cultures use fewer illustrators. The Arabs do not gesture or eat with the left hand as it is perceived as unclean. Members of some Asian countries refrain from patting the head, as the head is considered sacred.

Regulators are vocalics, kinesics, and oculesics to regulate the flow of conversation. As with emblems, they are also culture specific. Interruptions, for example, are regulators as is the use of silence. Brazilians interrupt twice as much as the British or Americans. In Bulgaria, when people nod their heads, it means no, but in other parts of the world, nodding means yes. The French also like to interrupt with interjections such as an exclamation, a remark, a protest, or even laughter. Pauses and filler cues such as "uh huh" (British) or "hai hai" (Japanese) are also regulators as is eye contact. Regulators, like other nonverbal gestures, have the potential to create misunderstandings when used across cultures.

Adaptors are essential postural changes at a low level of awareness. Seldom intentional, adaptors are often true indicators of what a person is thinking because people perform these movements at a subconscious level. For example, a slumped posture conveys boredom and disinterest, while an erect posture suggests enthusiasm and vitality. Similarly, leaning forward suggests keen listening and active involvement while leaning away indicates disinterest and boredom. Other examples of adaptors include fiddling with one's hair (low involvement), chewing fingernails (anxiety), tapping one's foot and leg (impatience), playing with jewelry (nervousness), and cracking knuckles (awkwardness).

Extent of eye contact and its implication in various cultures

Minimal or very less eye contact:	Far East Asian countries
Moderate eye contact:	Thailand, India, Pakistan, Korea, Africa
Firm eye contact:	United States, most parts of northern Europe, Turkey
Intense eye contact:	Saudi Arabia, Italy, Spain, Greece, parts of South America

Meaning of raised eyebrows in various cultures

Germans	Brilliant!
Arabs and Chinese	Disagreement

Impression Formation

Impression formation occurs throughout the process of communication. An individual's personality, physical attributes, profession, and behavior create an impression on the receiver. Positive impression formation is often related to the person's posture, style of walking, voice modulation, eye contact, dress, and accessories. However, norms regarding what constitutes professionalism vary across cultures. While some types of business attire are universally acceptable in all cultures, the same may not hold true for eye contact, voice modulation, and posture. In the United States, for example, assertiveness is a valued trait but this may not hold true for many South Asian countries. A positive impression in these countries is associated with passive behavior (especially when lower in hierarchy), a reserved communication style, and minimal display of gestures.

Interpreting Nonverbal Messages

Nonverbal messages must be interpreted in totality and not in isolation because most messages have more than one possible interpretation. Nonverbal messages are often rooted in cultural contexts. For example, it may appear perfectly normal in many cultures to lightly pat a child's head, but the gesture has a negative connotation in Thailand. Similarly, in some cultures, direct eye contact is preferred, while in others, a direct gaze is considered offensive. South European countries are more physically demonstrative than the north European countries.

In a negotiation process, the Americans erroneously concluded that the Chinese were in agreement with their proposal. Every time the Americans expressed a viewpoint, they were met with silence and an impassive gaze. Because there was no overt resistance, the Americans felt confident about their proposal. The confidence was misplaced, however.

Handshakes

It is important to consider the effects of cultural differences when inter-preting handshake cues. For example, in the Middle East, the grip is more gentle than executive in nature. In most Asian countries, direct eye contact is avoided when shaking hands. It is considered suspicious in the United States and in Latin American countries when people avoid eye contact while shaking hands. In Islamic countries, it is taboo to shake hands with women. Women also avoid touching gestures such as the shoulder pat. In the United States, women are accustomed to using the executive grip when shaking hands with both men and women. In India, businessmen also prefer the executive grip; however, only a few women use it; most women prefer the gentle touching of the fingers or the *limp fish* handshake, which can be misinterpreted in other cultures as a sign of weakness. In many countries including India, shoulder pats, kissing on the cheek, embraces, or other types of touching are considered a violation of one's personal space, especially between strangers. In Japan, the custom is to bow, although visiting dignitaries need not do so. U.S. President Obama was criticized by the U.S. media for bowing too low to the point of depicting extreme servility to his Japanese counterpart (see picture in the following text):

President Obama: Bowing too low?

Source: The Telegraph (2009).

U.S. President George Bush in 1992 toured Australia and gave a peace sign in the form of a *V* gesture to a group of farmers in Canberra. He apparently wanted to appease the farmers who were protesting U.S. farm subsidies. The signal backfired; the outward facing *V* sign in Australia is an insulting and hostile gesture.

Source: Tarpley and Chaitkin (2004).

North Americans, for example, value privacy; therefore they have fairly wide proxemic requirements in contrast to Latin Americans who have little concept of privacy. The British maintain greater distance than the French, who are a more high-contact culture than the former. Similarly, an Arab's concept of personal space is very different from that of an American (see the following illustration). As with other types of non-verbal communication, space and distance are open to misinterpretation and misunderstandings. A too-close proximity is often viewed as invading the privacy and space of another person. People tend to react, become defensive in their behavior, and actually move away from the person who they perceive as invading their space.

An Arab greeting an American

Preferred distances between people belonging to different cultures:

Least   Moderate   Most

⬅━━━━━━━━━━━━━━━━━━━━━━━━━━━━━━━━━━━➡

Arabs, Latin Americans, Greeks, Turks, French, Italians, Indians, Japanese, Chinese, Thai, British, Germans, Dutch, Americans

Hall distinguishes two types of spatial arrangements that can convey different types of meaning and hinder effective communication: the sociofugal space (greater distance between the manager and the subordinates expressed by placement of furniture and room arrangement), and the sociopetal arrangement (minimal distance between the manager and subordinates resulting from room and furniture arrangement).

Japanese office seating arrangements are designed to facilitate control and quick interpersonal communication. The manager sits in a far corner to supervise ably the subordinates who sit facing each other, each with a small desk. The manager's desk is slightly bigger than that of the subordinates. In the conference room, the seating is strictly hierarchical, with the manager sitting at the head of the table and the subordinates sitting in decreasing order of hierarchy.

Source: Nishiyama (2000).

Touching

Touching is a universal emotional behavior, though it differs widely in social contexts across cultures. Touching in the workplace can be indicative of positive emotions such as appreciation, support, affection, inclusion, and liking. Touching is also said to facilitate self-disclosure. In a multicultural workforce, opportunities for conflicts are imminent because each culture has its own norms regarding touching behavior.

With respect to touching, cultures may be divided into contact and noncontact cultures. In the workplace, touching behavior can be triggered by professional concerns (handshakes to greet people, the need to pat the back of a junior member to motivate or congratulate him or her); by concerns relating to politeness (light kiss on the cheek); or friendship (hugging, caressing). In many countries such as the United States, touching behavior at the workplace has become a matter of litigation. A senior who pokes his subordinate to emphasize a point is viewed as a bully; a casual pat on the arm may be (mis)construed as sexual misconduct or harassment.

For example, at the G-8 Summit in St. Petersburg in 2006, U.S. President George Bush stepped behind the German Chancellor, Angela Merkel, and gave her shoulders a brief massage. Visibly surprised and

George Bush and Angela Merkel: Too close for comfort?

Source: Warren (2006).

plainly uncomfortable, Merkel threw up her arms to avoid Bush's hands. The event was captured by the press and attracted a lot of negative attention on websites and other social media. In Germany, surprisingly, the reaction was mute and one of indifference. The debate was branded as more of an American rather than a German issue. Needless to say, in the United States, an offense of this type could result in litigation (See the previous illustration).

In another incident, Iranian President Mahmoud Ahmadinejad was criticized severely by the Islamic clerics for hugging the mother of Venezuelan President Hugo Chavez at his funeral in Caracas. Under Islamic law, it is strictly forbidden for a man to have physical contact with a member of the female gender, who is not closely related to him.

"Shaking hands with a non-mahram (non-family member) woman, whether young or old, and under any circumstances, is not allowed. Hugging or expressing emotions is improper for the dignity of the president of a country such as the Islamic Republic of Iran," Mohammad Taghi Rahbar told Iran's Mehr News Agency.

Source: Associated Press (2013).

Members of contact cultures maintain closer distance, face each other, and tend to touch each other while conversing. Members of noncontact cultures tend to maintain distance with each other and rarely touch each other during conversation. These differences can create communication problems. The latter's behavior may appear cold and distant to those from high-contact cultures who in turn may perceive them as pushy and aggressive.

> In 2009, there was an apparent breach of protocol when Mrs. Obama briefly put her hand on the back of Queen Elizabeth II as they chatted at a reception. British etiquette is rigid about protocol (touching the Queen is a strict no-no).
>
> *Source*: Chua-Eoan (2009).

Handling a business card in some cultures such as Japan is akin to a touching gesture. The card has to be held in both hands and read carefully for its contents. It is considered discourteous to write anything on the card, fold it, or put in the pocket or bag without glancing at it.

Summary

1. It is vital to increase one's understanding of global norms of etiquette before attempting to do business beyond boundaries.
2. Nonverbal communication is a product of culture and tends to be interpreted in a culture-specific way. Deciphering nonverbal communication is a crucial skill for anyone working across cultures.
3. Technically, the study of body language includes kinesics, oculesics, proxemics, haptics, vocalics, and chronemics.
4. People use kinesics and oculesics to manage their conversations with each other.
5. Kinesics comprises emblems, illustrators, regulators, and adaptors, and each of these has a specific communication objective.
6. In a multicultural workplace, people may send negative micromessages to members of minority or ethnic groups (people who are perceived to be different from the majority), even if their verbal messages are polite and courteous. This form of communication complicates

relationships and provides an unconscious source of misunderstandings across cultures. It also has the potential to affect performance and output.

Key Terms

- Conscious and subliminal messages
- Kinesics, oculesics, haptic, chronemics, and vocalics
- Illustrators, regulators, and adaptors

CHAPTER 5

Influence of National Culture, Corporate Culture, and Multinational Culture on Intercultural Communication

Since intercultural encounters are as old as humanity, multinational business is as old as organized state

—Hofstede (2001:440)

Introduction

A multinational company (MNC) is one that has operations other than marketing in more than one country. An MNC operates across markets, nations, and cultures. The units of an MNC are dispersed across national borders to reap the benefits of the availability of raw materials and access to untapped resources, markets, and new customers. The activities of an MNC may involve sales, manufacturing, asset allocation, and human resource management, as well as operations. The business of the company is conducted in areas other than the country of origin. MNCs diffuse practices across borders and have the potential to drive change as a result of their ability to integrate operations across distinct national systems. The extent of the diffusion, however, is shaped by the culture of the host country of operation.

Because MNCs operate in a sociocultural environment at times vastly different from their own country, there are bound to be challenging inter-cultural encounters. These encounters may or may not lead to mutual understanding, as each group tries to protect its cultural identity and hold on to prejudices and stereotypes. This phenomenon led to the idea that organizations need to have a distinct culture, which is separate from the cultures of their employees; thus, the notion of organizational climate and, later on, corporate culture was born.

Scholars agree that organizational or corporate culture is distinct from national culture. Culture is a holistic system, comprising parts and sub-parts. It is socially constructed, is of an enduring nature, and includes cultural symbols (Hofstede 2005). National culture is absorbed in the first 10 years of one's life and is influenced greatly by the family and the school. National culture, to a large degree, forms the basic values of the individual.

Corporate culture is acquired culture and consists of organizational practices that are amenable to change. The term refers to the values rooted in the organization and how these values influence the behavior and attitude of the employees working in the organization. The values of the corporate culture manifest themselves in the organization's vision and mission statements, product design, logos, packaging, and workplace policies.

A flash strike occurred in 2008 at the Cadbury Schweppes plc plant, Nigeria. Workers wore their uniforms inside out. Nigeria is home to the traditional Yoruba culture where wearing attire inside out is considered a bad omen and a symbol of protest, a warning, defeat, or mourning for the loss of a leader (Oba). Superstition also held that wearing one's attire inside out would bring the wearer good luck. The union leader in Cadbury (Nigeria) used this symbolic behavior to "win the struggle." The British expatriate's directors found this act "funny, amazing, ridiculous and unacceptable." In another case, the British managers were surprised that the Nigerian employees found it difficult to address their British seniors by name. They would use their position instead (for example, MD for Managing Director; OD for Operations Director). George would be called IO (Intelligence Officer) rather than by his first name.

Source: George and Owoyemi (2012).

In his research, Hofstede concluded that the management practices used successfully in the West such as Herzberg's theory, Maslow's theory, and theories X and Y might not be applicable outside the boundaries of the United States, mainly because of the differences in culture (Hofstede 1980). The national culture of the host country will always be a useful point of reference for multinational organizations desirous of doing business outside their borders (Hofstede 2005).

Each organization can be categorized by one of the following three descriptors concerning how business is conducted:

1. Ethnocentric: In this situation, the organization seeks to duplicate the home culture in the host country.
2. Polycentric: In this situation, the organization's operations are handed over to the local or the host country.
3. Geocentric: In this situation, the multinational subsidiaries and the host country are seen as parts of a whole with an integrated global outlook; each unit's culture is distinct.

Communication and the Organization

The success of an MNC is the result of effective and efficient integration of its global resources in a multinational, multilingual, and multicultural environment. This is achieved through setting up systems to facilitate the transfer of knowledge and norms of interaction across boundaries.

Mr. Kamal Atal, Indian, working in the international finance division of a prominent Dubai hotel

"To be able to conduct business, expatriates need to adjust to the local culture. I am from India and initially I did have problems relating to the new environment. Today I can confidently say that I am truly multicultural. I am meeting people belonging to different nationalities and I can successfully gauge how best to deal with them. Patience, tact, and perseverance are important qualities for expatriates and guest workers for achieving success in a global environment."

Transfer of Knowledge

The traditional sender–receiver model of communication is the foundation of the knowledge transfer process. In an MNC, the knowledge transfer takes place through various means and not just through human communication. It may be coded via abstract forms such as data and objects.

Since the management of knowledge is dependent on the location of the organization, dissemination is strongly influenced by contextual factors (such as the culture of the organization, language ability of the sender and receiver, perceived cultural distance, and the like). It is also true that organizations per se do not have a cultural baggage, but its employees do. People are often slaves of their thought processes, habits, and ways of doing things. These elements can be barriers to knowledge transfer, even between employees of the same subsidiary. Many MNCs send expatriates to their local subsidiaries to manage global operations and to facilitate effective communication between the headquarters (HQ) and the subsidiaries.

Shared language between the MNC HQ and the subsidiaries increases understanding. According to experts, the biggest barrier to knowledge sharing between an MNC and its subsidiaries is the lack of concordance between the national culture of the host country and the parent country of the organization. Successful cross-cultural relationships are heavily dependent on the degree of cultural distance.

The learning style of the sender also impacts on the extent of knowledge transfer and retention. The acquisition of knowledge from employees, suppliers, clients, subcontractors, and competitors facilitate the learning process, and are influenced by the culture of the organization. The process of learning and teaching is also influenced by the cultural background of the learner and the teacher. Predominant learning styles vary across cultures. Some cultures encourage active participant-centered learning, while others advocate the merits of teacher-centered learning in which the role of the student is passive. This difference has the potential to affect the knowledge-sharing propensity of the individuals.

Cultural openness enables a person to engage in meaningful interactions with people belonging to another culture and improve the process of knowledge transfer. Cultural openness indicates a high level of cultural quotient (popularly known as CQ) and implies that the person has a high level of tolerance, respect for others, appreciates differences, and has a desire to improve interpersonal communication.

Communication Structures to Support Subsidiary Roles

Research on MNCs and their global operations seems to suggest that most of the intangible assets are no longer situated in the HQ, but in the subsidiaries located in various countries. This is the primary reason why effective interactions between the MNC's HQ and its subsidiaries are so crucial. Appropriately designed communication networks assist in facilitating both internal as well as external communication. Ethnocentric management can no longer be perceived as the best management strategy; MNCs have to accommodate the autonomous culture of its subsidiaries to realize any long-term gain, considering the vast physical as well as cultural distance.

The MNC may assume one of the following roles depending on the capabilities of the subsidiaries.

Subsidiary as a strategic partner

The subsidiary is very capable and its operations are strategic to the MNC. In this case, the subsidiary

1. actively contributes to the planning, organization, and coordination of the MNC;
2. is involved in the problem-solving and decision-making activities of the MNC;
3. is likely to possess its own R&D division and contribute to product and market development.

Possible communication approach: highly networked; high level of information sharing; tactical, operational, and strategic synergy; managers of both the HQ and subsidiary are fully informed about all managerial activities.

Subsidiary as contributor

The subsidiary provides a valuable resource input and operates in a relatively niche or less critical market area. In this case

- the subsidiary is at best a source of a valuable asset;
- its strength needs to be leveraged for long-term gains.

Possible communication approach: moderately networked; intermittent communication; operational synergy; managers need not be involved in or informed of all the decision making and planning processes.

Subsidiary as an implementer

The subsidiary operates in a market of relatively little importance to the MNC. In this case, the subsidiary is merely an implementer of the MNC's policies and plans.

Possible communication approach: very low level of networking; at best tactical synergy; infrequent communication; managers are far removed from decision making and planning processes.

Subsidiary as a black hole

If the MNC feels that a presence is necessary in an emerging market or in a highly competitive market environment, it may establish a small subsidiary unit to gather information and utilize the potential of the local market, even though the chances of profitability are very limited.

- The subsidiary managers are good opportunity identifiers.
- Key liaison official interacts with local suppliers and dealers.

In their paper "Role-Related Communication Structures and Strategies in MNCs," authors Tuija Mainela and Timo Mustonen conclude that full-scale subsidiaries typically desire far greater autonomy from the MNCs and they often complain about the lack of a shared view of development directions.

Source: Mainela and Mustonen (2008).

Possible communication approach: reasonably networked; regular communication; moderate strategic, operational, and tactical synergy; managers involved in knowledge transfer.

Internal Communication and MNCs

Communication issues are significant in MNCs. The presence of subsidiaries across far-flung countries with different cultures complicates effective communication. The function of corporate communication in such situations is to ensure communication across all levels and in all subsidiaries in a uniformly coherent manner.

Heterogeneity and diversity characterize most MNC operations. Thus, internal communication is likely to be difficult for the following reasons:

- Geographical distance among the subsidiaries
- Time difference between the subunit and the HQ
- Differences in language skills
- Cultural distance between the subunits
- Ineffective or weak regulation of information flow
- Ethnocentric orientation of the parent company

Communication type

Communication may be of several types: (1) task-focused communication (instructions, memos, meetings, proposals, reports, etc.), (2) information-centric communication (information related to current developments, or training and development needs related to information sharing), (3) directive communication (information related to goal setting, targets, budgets, manuals, etc.), (4) change communication (sharing change expectations with employees), (5) media communication (communicating with external stakeholders), and finally, (6) cultural communication (leadership development, gaining support for shared vision and values, etc.).

Methods of communication may be oral or written and typically include face-to-face meetings, presentations, podcasts, teleconferencing and e-mails, memos, twitter, CEO blog, or company newsletter.

Communication strategy

Answering the following questions will provide a beginning for the MNC to develop an effective communication strategy:

- Why (purpose): the goal of the communication (to inform, persuade, or motivate)
- What (content): direct or indirect formats depending on the message and circumstances
- To whom (audience): the characteristics and preferences of the target
- How (technique): availability of technology; channels of communication
- When (timing)
- Where (location)
- Who (responsibility for sending messages and receiving feedback)

In low-context cultures, the verbal content of a message is of greater value than the medium of the message delivery. In high-context cultures, a high premium is placed on face-to-face interactions; the context or setting, along with a large number of nonverbal cues, conveys deeper meaning than the literal words of a message.

Effect of Cultural Differences in Communication and Feedback Styles

Research supports the concept that adaptation of local employees to the MNC is improved as more information is provided to them. However, even in routine communications, care has to be taken to customize the communication. For example, feedback behavior differs across cultures. In high-context, relationship-centered cultures, feedback is implicit and situation specific. It is given indirectly so as to maintain harmony and relationships. In contrast, feedback is more explicit and person specific in low-context cultures that value results and performance over people. It is therefore given directly.

In her first assignment abroad (New Delhi), Sally, the assistant manager at a global firm, was set to receive feedback from her Indian manager at the annual performance appraisal interview. After the hour-long session, Sally was still unclear as to what was expected of her, where she had gone wrong, and how to improve future performance. When she requested information concerning two or three key areas where she was found wanting, the manager seemed to praise her efforts by saying the upper management found her to be very responsible. Yet the supervisor later asked her if "it could be possible for her to at times remain after 6 p.m. to complete pending work." Sally could not determine whether this was a command, a request, or an option that she had! The manager even went on to say that assertiveness was a very valued asset, but requested her to be even more polite (than she already was) to the local dealers! It was only when conversing with the vice president that Sally understood that she needed to work on two things to be successful at her new workplace: to be a shade less assertive and to agree to work beyond stipulated hours at certain times.

Management of expatriates

Globalization is forcing companies to learn how to operate more efficiently. A major component of efficiency is the effective deployment and management of international human resources.

Even as the global economic downturn continued, the Global Relocation Trends Survey 2012 reported that growth in the number of international assignments by multinational companies increased nearly 50 percent from the previous year. In spite of "regional economic woes," multinational companies continue to deploy workers in merging and developing markets.

Source: ASTD Staff (2012).

Since an international assignment is a costly business per person, it is important that the returns are cost effective and viable. A few studies report that predeparture trainings prior to the international assignment contribute little to the expatriate adjustment, focused as they are on simulations and lectures. Still others report that some exposure via such trainings is better than no exposure at all. Key attributes of a successful expatriate manager include the ability to balance the needs of the parent company and the host company.

In Thailand, for example, knowledge of the local language is crucial to building relationships with local businessmen. An expatriate is expected to know the concepts of *jai* (heart) such as *nam jai* (friendliness) as well as *kreang jai* (caution with words and action; empathy). Saving face and losing face are important concepts to appreciate to be able to work in Thailand.

Expatriate managers should ideally be dual citizens. This dual loyalty would help them to not only implement policies of the parent organization in the subsidiary but also transfer meaningful knowledge about the subsidiary to the parent company (Figure 5.1).

Communication is most effective when managers with a particular commitment profile are matched with the appropriate assignments in the subsidiary. Adapting to the audience and the context are key components of any effective communication strategy, and they are certainly critical for multinational assignments.

Dual citizens	Go native
High allegiance to parent company and new company	High allegiance to only the new company
Desirable role in subsidiary: STRATEGIST	Desirable role in subsidiary: CONTRIBUTOR
Hearts at home	Free agent
High allegiance to only the parent company	Allegiance to neither the parent company nor the new company
Desirable role in subsidiary: IMPLEMENTER	Not a desirable trait

Figure 5.1 Matching commitment profile of expatriate managers with appropriate assignment in a subsidiary

Improve communication skills

Share values of the parent organization

Observe behavior

Communicate roles of expatriates in the subsidiary

Develop social networking skills: Share knowledge—transfer of information to and from the parent

Language training facilitates effectiveness in communication especially on foreign shores. Training often consists of workshops on giving and receiving instructions, listening skills, and interpersonal skills. While a working knowledge of English is always desirable, it is hardly spoken in many countries. Language tends to exclude outsiders, who may face many language barriers in communicating with the local clients and customers.

Communication practices in Indian culture include implicit communication, indirectness, passive and aggressive centeredness, relationship focus, and respect for age and position in hierarchy. These characteristics create communication barriers between Indians and Westerners especially in interpersonal relationships. Because English is an official language in India, the communication challenge is not as severe as in China or Japan. In China, age is venerated; older and more experienced Chinese may expect younger expatriates to respect their authority. Cultural practices such as "face" also creates misunderstandings. The lack of *guanxi*, sustained relationship building, as it is called in China, also creates communication barriers with Westerners. While documents may be translated into English, the same cannot be said of oral communication especially with suppliers, vendors, and distributors whose knowledge of English is quite limited.

Even in one's own culture, instances reveal that communication is rarely ideal unless the sender or the receiver or both are sensitive and adaptive to each other. When interacting with a member of an unfamiliar culture, the problem is compounded because so little is known about the other person. Familiar scripts do not work, and misunderstandings can occur if additional effort is not made to understand the other's cultural

A survey of 210 Chinese managers by researchers Heffernan and Crawford in 2001 suggested that some elements of Confucianism are weakening due to exposure to and even adoption of Western lifestyles. However, three core Confucian values remain important: kindness, temperance (including harmony), and perseverance.

Source: Goodall and Warner (2007).

leanings. The widely available communication guidelines on the Internet with a list of dos and don'ts will not guarantee success unless a concerted effort is made by the organization and the expatriate managers to overcome ethnocentrism (the belief that one's own culture is superior to others).

In the accompanying Figure 5.2, the person on the left (A) represents the expatriate's home culture and the person on the right (B) represents the culture of the subsidiary. Communication is in harmony when A has an understanding of B's background by reading about the other culture; taking part in preassignment training on how the people of this culture communicate; interacting with others of the culture to gain insight; and learning the local language. With this preparation, the chances of successful communication are greatly increased; A would likely now have a high CQ and exhibit cultural intelligence. Gradually, the expatriate starts appreciating the market fundamentals of the subsidiary as well. Relational exchanges translate into economic benefits and reciprocity, the basis of effective communication.

Interviews of Western expatriates revealed that many found management employees in most Asian countries to be lacking in expressive

Person A   Person B

Figure. 5.2 Maintaining harmony in expatriate Communication

communication skills. They tended to say what they perceived their bosses wanted to hear, thus distorting the process of communication as well as decision making. Most expatriates agreed that the Asian managers tended to tell harmless lies (for instance, as arriving late to the office because of traffic jams when they had actually overslept). What Western expatriates saw as big problems (reporting late for a scheduled meeting, for instance) was often viewed by the Asian managers as minor hiccups. Errors in the instructions were not considered as professional *hara-kiri*; when errors occurred, they would just correct them. Expatriates also acknowledged that the educational systems in most Asian countries did not encourage questioning and assertive skills.

Dealing with International Communication Problems

International communication problems can be minimized when both the expatriate and the local employee make strides to overcome their cultural differences.

Guidelines for Expatriates

- Develop initial awareness about the other culture. It is important to develop a positive attitude about the new culture and its inhabitants and steer clear from prejudices and stereotypes. Postpone judgments about the locals and smile genuinely.
- Learn to accurately interpret the nonverbal conventions of the other culture, including gestures, silence, eye contact, head nods, and facial expressions.
- Know the rules regarding paying and receiving compliments, offering and accepting apologies, giving instructions, and making requests.
- Elicit frequent feedback from the local employees to check their understanding of the task assigned to them. Do not assume that the assigned task will be completed as desired. Provide frequent opportunities for the local employees to make suggestions about how to improve internal communication.

- Follow up periodically on the task assigned to avoid delay in completion.
- Immerse in the culture of the other. Develop social networking skills to truly understand people and their customs. Socialize and mingle with the locals, eat the food they eat, and try to learn a few important words of their language.
- Rely on personal experiences to build a bond. Share experiences and ask for clarifications. A liaison officer or a mediator may be helpful in learning to understand the local people and the subsidiary market.
- Use voice and tone mindfully. This is true for both written as well as oral communication. Loud and aggressive tones may be perceived as being too harsh by the other culture.

Guidelines for Local Employees (Especially Those Belonging to Asian Countries) When Dealing with Expatriates

- Try to develop a working knowledge of English. This will help improve understanding of instructions.
- Improve writing and presentation skills, especially in English.
- Learn to recognize differences in the working style of expatriates that visit the country. For instance, understand that Germans in general are detailed and meticulous in their approach; the French are direct in their communication, and Americans are task oriented.
- Understand that expatriates will naturally be paid a higher compensation because of the nature of their assignment. Accept that differences may exist in age and gender expectations (a senior local manager reporting to a younger expatriate manager or male managers reporting to a female expatriate manager).
- Learn to be explicit, especially when dealing with Westerners. Communicate the message upfront and give clear verbal and nonverbal signals that they can understand (saying no, expressing disagreement, or nodding for agreement).

- Understand that Westerners do not relate respect with relationship building, consensus management, and group-think. They place a premium on task performance, and for them, respect is related to the deliverables expected from the employees.
- Practice assertiveness when dealing with Western expatriate managers who like employees to speak up at meetings.
- Learn to speak with concrete evidence such as facts, data, and statistics.
- Make copies of important documents as records.

Expatriate managers and employees alike may benefit from training in business etiquette and time management as it relates to the other culture. Following the stated guidelines, expatriate and local managers will begin to succeed in communicating with one another. As both sides exhibit maturity and cultural understanding, connecting with one another will become more natural.

Summary

1. MNCs diffuse practices across borders and have the potential to drive change as a result of their ability to integrate operations across distinct national systems.
2. The extent of the diffusion, however, is shaped by the culture of the host country of operation.
3. The success of an MNC is the result of effective and efficient integration of its global resources in a multinational, multilingual, and multicultural environment.
4. Research supports the concept that adaptation of local employees to the MNC is improved as more information is provided to them. However, even in routine communications, care has to be taken to customize the communication.
5. Communication is most effective when managers with a particular commitment profile are matched with the appropriate assignment in the subsidiary.

6. International communication problems can be minimized when both the expatriate and the local employee make strides to overcome their cultural differences.

Key Terms

- Host country
- Subsidiary roles
- Ethnocentric, polycentric, and geocentric organizations

CHAPTER 6

Communication in Cross Border Mergers and Acquisitions

A merger is like a river flowing into the sea. When the tides are changing the boats do not know exactly how to align. Then progressively they manage to do so...

—Jerome Granboulan, Vice President,
Arcelor Mittal, in McKinsey Quarterly, 2008

Introduction

Mergers across cross borders are usually associated with additional frictions. Challenges include cultural, territorial, and communication differences that have the potential to increase the cost of merging the two firms. Differences in governance standards, legal requirements, and market considerations can also stall processes and make adjustment difficult.

Mergers and acquisitions (M&As) are intended to spur growth, improve competitiveness, and allow movement into previously unchartered territories. The KPMG M&A Predictor report for July 2012 showed a decline in M&As, which is likely due to a number of factors, including economic cooling in China, financial problems in Europe, and continued deleveraging in the global financial sector. Many companies underestimate the possible complications that can arise out of a poorly executed merger. According to KPMG,

- in 34 percent of the mergers, business costs have increased;
- only 20 percent of the companies have achieved some of their objectives in the process of M&As;
- of the new companies created from mergers, 57 percent are lagging behind their competitors;

- in 61 percent of the cases, shareholders suffered losses due to the fact that investments in M&As did not pay off as anticipated.

Companies often fall short of their goals in the M&A process due in part to failure to acknowledge the important role of culture, communication, and employee buy-in. Some of the aftereffects of an unsuccessful merger include high employee turnover; problems in morale, productivity, and communication; and high absenteeism. Companies are only now talking about culture fit, communication, value systems, and other "soft" issues that were previously brushed aside or considered minimal considerations in a potential merger. Companies are now compelled to recognize the merits of cultural integration over mere financial and operational integration. While the latter is easy to accomplish, the former is less tangible; yet, it has the potential to topple the merged entity.

It is only natural that employees, suppliers, and customers feel anxious when a merger is announced. Cross border acquisitions and mergers create significant uncertainty; they entail not only coping with a new culture but also understanding a set of novel administrative, legal, market, and operational contexts.

Soon after a merger, it is important for the parent company to culturally integrate with the acquired company. The first step should be to analyze the differences in cultures, identify the barriers to communication, and draft an appropriate communication strategy. Ronald S. Burt, Hobart W. Williams Professor of Sociology and Strategy at the University of Chicago Graduate School of Business, recommends examining the corporate culture of the potential partner firm before considering a merger and to investigate the following:

1. The style of management in the firm: What vision and mission guides the thinking of the firm? How are the values promoted among the employees of the firm?
2. The relationship of the corporate culture to the market structure: If the market structure is dynamic, integration is easier because performance of the firm is independent of the culture of the firm.

Case I
Arcelor Mittal: Broken Promises?

In June 2006, the world's largest steel company was created with the merger of the France-based Arcelor and the India-based Mittal, forming Arcelor Mittal.

The process was far from amiable. The management of Arcelor was extremely hostile to the bid from Mittal Steels from the beginning. The French CEO was quick to dismiss Mittal Steel as a company of Indians and unworthy of "acquiring a European company." Support from the French government was also not forthcoming. Arcelor's management was deeply concerned about the possible layoff of 28,000 of the company's employees, despite repeated assurances by Mittal. The government of Luxemburg (a stakeholder) was also against the merger for many reasons. The key challenge was related to the integration of human resources. Internal communication and external communication were planned systematically, and the following series of steps were taken by the company with respect to communication.

Internal Communication

- Line managers were involved in the planning process to discuss the positive effects of the merger within their respective teams.
- The company introduced a website accessible to employees that included links to interviews with senior executives concerning the merger.
- A well-structured message was crafted to explain to the employees the details and the significance of the merger and the goal and objective of the merged entity.
- The management communicated with the employees in a focused manner; messages of a generic nature were deliberately avoided.
- The new entity—Arcelor Mittal—was launched in a grand ceremony, which was attended by the top 500 managers.
- Partnered with training companies and business schools to deliver training via traditional face-to-face programs and online courses; thousands enrolled in the English language courses.

External Communication

- The company launched a top-management road show that visited all major plant sites and cities, with company executives talking with the local employees and managers.
- Media interviews were conducted to convey the Arcelor Mittal message.

- *Media day* was held in Brussels, where presentations were made on the state of the merger. The media were invited to visit the various sites and report on the progress.
- Customized information was provided to the clients and customers about the advantages of the merger.

Current situation

Sometimes, merger teams succumb to politics and power, and integration can falter. Consider the following news report aired in November 2012 on the British Broadcasting Corporation (BBC) channel: The industry minister of France accused Arcelor Mittal of lying and urged it to leave France. "We do not want Mittal in France because they do not respect France," he was quoted by *Les Echos*, a financial newspaper. The outburst came after Arcelor Mittal announced it had postponed the relighting of a blast furnace at a plant in Dunkirk. "The problem of the blast furnaces at Florange is not the blast furnaces at Florange, its Mittal," said the industry minister.

A later news report (November 3, 2013) stated that Arcelor Mittal reported a narrower loss as compared to 2012. Its weakest area continued to be Europe where it had the highest production and the largest number of employees (http://corporate.arcelormittal.com/news-and-media/press-releases/2013).

Case II
Chrysler and Daimler Benz:
Failure to Unite the Cultural Divide

It was Daimler that proposed the merger. The merger of German Daimler Benz with U.S. Chrysler was announced in 1998 and touted as the "merger of equals," even though Daimler Benz acquired Chrysler for $38 billion. For companies as different from each other as Daimler and Chrysler, it was imperative that prior to the merger and immediately afterward, the culture fit had to be thought out completely. A thorough evaluation of the leadership style, communication approaches, and HR strategies of each company was needed. However, communication breakdown resulted in conflicts, which could not be managed well, as appropriate strategies had not been identified to resolve conflicts arising from cultural differences.

Two critical components of communication were missing in the newly formed company: trust and coordination. As a result of this lack, rumors and speculation were rife at the factories and the plants. The very phrase *merger of equals* was misleading, as the intent of Daimler Benz was essentially hostile—to dominate Chrysler. Had Daimler been honest about the deal and its intentions, mistrust could have been replaced with support and cooperation. Coordination, another key component of communication, was lacking. Each company was given the freedom to pursue its own direction initially, and this caused resentment among the respective employees. The opportunity to create cross company communication was lost as synergy was never really realized.

The Scene in 1998

Stallkamp, the North American President kept his employees informed about the merger through mass meetings, Chrysler's internal television network and newspaper, and by answering e-mail questions. In one month alone, he got 1,000 e-mails from concerned company employees. The questions and concerns reflected the range of issues, from the mundane to the significant, that needed to be worked out in one of the largest industrial mergers ever attempted. Employees questioned the kind of English that would be used. "There's American English and European English," Stallkamp said. "I got one e-mail from one of our employees on what's the proper way to spell tire: *t-i-r-e* or *t-y-r-e*?" But while some Chrysler employees may have fretted about what type of English they would have to use (American), most wouldn't have had to learn German. "The real issue is, there are 400,000 people or so on the other side who have to learn English," Stallkamp said. "For everything that's an issue here, there is an issue on the other side that we need to be aware of." (Akre 1998).

Even though efforts were made by the management to communicate with employees concerning the details of the integration process, cultural issues were too overwhelming. The merger was plagued by a series of lawsuits. In 2005, the chairman, J. E. Schrempp, resigned in response to the falling share prices following the transaction. Chrysler cars were not selling mainly due to Daimler's reluctance to invest in its machinery. In 2007, Daimler divested itself of Chrysler through a sell-off.

Table 6.1 Cultural and communication differences between the Americans and the Germans

S. no.	Chrysler	Daimler Benz
1	Open culture: Employees were free to express their views. Cross functional teams were in place. A culture of debate and discussion existed.	Closed culture: Hierarchical and top down management style was practiced. A culture of formality and discipline existed.
2	Risk oriented: Viewed as daring, diverse, and creative, Americans are known for their entrepreneurial spirit and innovativeness.	Risk averse: Viewed as conservative, efficient, and safe, Germans are known for their precision and rule-bound approach.
3	Liberal spending: Management demanded high salaries and travel by first class.	Conservative spending: Management was generally conservative about salaries. Focused on savings rather than spending on luxuries (like traveling first class).
4	Timing of news release: Conflict about release of news of the merger; Americans wanted it in their time zone.	Timing of news release: Planned to release the news of the merger at a time appropriate to the European media.
5	Casual dress and behavior: Adopted casual dress code and language at the workplace.	Formal dress and behavior: Adhered to suit-and-tie dress code and respected titles and designation in the workplace.
6	Shared decision making: Lower management involved in the decision making.	Centralized decision making: Decisions taken by the top management only.
7	Brand image: Attractive, eye-catching design at a very competitive price.	Brand image: Customer proposition—quality and precision.
8	Development model: Adopted trial and error method for reaching solutions.	Development model: Drafted detailed and intricate plans.

Case III
The Case of Cisco Systems: Model for M&A communication

Three principles guide Cisco System's postmerger integration—alignment, communication, and operational effectiveness. The merger of Cisco-StrataCom and Cerent was a successful one. Integration teams were created to oversee integration and alignment activities. Standard procedures were adopted to enable rapid and consistent collaboration processes. Attention was focused by the integration team on clarity of roles, dependencies, responsibilities, deliverables, and timelines for the large number of integration tasks planned for each of the departments. Each department had a set of well-defined guidelines to facilitate the integration process in a smooth manner. The CEO of Cisco Systems,

John Chambers, institutionalized the motto "communicate early, often, and honestly." In terms of communication,

- a buddy system was created in the first phase of integration so that employees (of the acquired company) had someone to go to for resolving their questions and anxieties;
- orientation meetings were held with employees to address concerns regarding the merger;
- standard information sharing and collaboration tools such as Cisco Unified Meeting Place, WebEx (for online meetings), audio conference calls, telepresence (video conference calls), e-mails, online document sharing, and project management software were used to conduct work;
- qualitative and quantitative metrics were used to track integration efforts.

Case IV
Tata Steel and Corus Merger: Leadership, Culture, or Communication?

In the year 2008, Indian Tata steel acquired the Anglo Dutch steel firm Corus for $11.3 billion, making it the biggest acquisition by an Indian firm in history. The Tata Steel–Corus merger was vulnerable to cultural as well as ego clashes that resulted from the dynamics of cross border integration. Standard & Poor had assigned a negative rating to Tata in April 2007, in part due to the belief that Indians firms lacked expertise in cross border M&As. Support was lacking from the British trade union leaders who warned about the potential downfall of the U.K. steel industry if the merger took place. Following the recommendations of experts to "go slow on the post integration strategies," Tata Steel did the following:

- Allowed the existing management to continue and to also assist in the postmerger integration plans. A roadmap was created to guide the company through the integration process.
- Created cross functional teams with timelines for each integration activity.
- Communicated the progress of the integration to the larger organization (including the merged entity) via e-mails,

seminars, and meetings, so that employees were positive and upbeat about the changes. The management also communicated to the employees of the acquired company the beliefs and value systems of the acquiring company.

- Created forums for resolving concerns and anxieties with respect to the merger.
- Hired the services of Communicaid, Europe's leading culture and communication consulting firm, to launch a series of cultural awareness programs on "Doing Business with India" for senior Corus professionals (Table 6.2).

Table 6.2 Cultural and communication differences between the British and the Indians

S. no.	Tata Group (Indian)	Corus (British)
1	Culture of underachievement: Indian way of life: a little underachievement is an acceptable cultural trait	Culture of achievement: British managers are unwilling to promise more that they feel that can deliver. They feel it is better not to take on a target which might take them outside their comfort zone
2	Company controls private time: In India, managers are used to being available 7 days a week. Even on holidays one is supposed to be available by phone.	Private time is sacred: In Britain and much of western Europe, private time is sacred; after 4pm Friday until Sunday there is little chance of the company being able to contact them.
3	Loyalty is paramount: It is still difficult to fire people in India, in spite of how poorly they perform.	Performance is paramount: In Britain and northern Europe, performance is more important than loyalty.
4	Indirect assignment: In India when a manager wants a job done by someone, the expected way to approach the worker is to 'request' the action or to seek a 'favor' even if the person is responsible for the work.	Direct assignment: In Britain, job descriptions are clearly demarcated. One is supposed to do what one is assigned to. When a manager wants work done, it is acceptable to state simply' "Please do this'.
5	Conflict avoidance: When dealing with stakeholders, government, or the community,- the focus is to build relationships and reciprocity rather than stir conflict.	Conflict normalcy: Rules and guidelines are followed even when dealing with stakeholders. Conflict is considered healthy and part of doing business.
6	Diversity acceptance: Better at accepting diversity.-.Typically speak at least two or three languages-mother tongue, a regional dialect, and the English language. Focus is on accepting differences and working on similarities	Diversity avoidance: Exposed to a single lingua franca. Do not easily embrace differences, and some have been accused of racism at times.

7	High context: Belong to the high context culture category.	Low context: Categorized as a low context culture.
8	Polychromic: Efficiently multitask which may be seen as procrastination and deadline avoidance. Not very punctual. Frequently interrupt. Perform well under pressure.	Monochromic: Concentrate on a single task at a time. Task and process oriented. Committed to schedules and deadlines. Highly punctual. Schedule appointments and plan accordingly.
9	Amenable to change and adaptability.	Resistant to change and do not adapt easily.
10	Team-oriented and group motivated. An individual's achievement is tied to group promotion.	Individualistic in orientation.
11	Nonassertive. Somewhat masculine, but helpful and affectionate.	Assertive: Masculine, rule bound approach.
12	Tolerate ambiguity reasonably well.	Tolerate ambiguity reasonably well.

The Current Situation

The merger integration did not start on a positive note. Adams, who had replaced Varin as the CEO, in 2009, left in 2010. Unionism was at its peak at that time. A slowdown had started, and job cuts were on the increase. Two senior management professionals were sent from India to stem the tide; one returned because he felt that his recommendations were not taken seriously. U.K. Chaturvedi stayed on, and under his leadership Corus Strip Products (CSP) had started generating profits of $400 million by 2011. However, Chaturvedi was moved from CSP and made the Chief Technical Officer to work under Karl-Ulrich Köhler, a steel veteran from the German company ThyssenKrupp. Chaturvedi resigned in January 2012 citing lack of freedom to take decisions. Köhler, the third managing director in two years, advocated centralization of processes and functions.

Communication was compromised, and it is alleged that he surrounded himself with yes-men. There was no British manager in the top management team led by Koehler. The decision was made to call in consulting firms, which cost the company $80 million. But, says a former executive, "The consultants left when it was time to deliver." As a result, production at Tata was down by 30 percent, and liabilities continued to grow. Corus badly needs to put its act together" (Thomas 2013). Countries have legal requirements in place for M&As (see Appendix B, which has a short note on this).

Summary

1. Communication is an essential prerequisite for efficiently integrating the businesses of the two companies in cross border mergers.

2. The major challenge in cross border mergers is to overcome barriers caused by differences in culture.

3. Rapid integration is vital to the success of the merger. Things have to work quickly; this leads to better cross functional synergy and realization of earnings. Effective communication, however, must be an ongoing process that continues after the integration process is completed, at least for the next five years.

4. Key employees of the acquired firm must also be involved in the integration and communication exercise process.

5. Mentoring of employees in the acquired firm can assist them in dealing with postmerger stress and anxiety-related issues.

6. A conscious strategy for integrated corporate communication is essential. This strategy should include how messages and appeals will be addressed coherently across brands, markets, suppliers, clients, and external and internal customers.

7. Continuous communication with employees is essential during the integration process.

8. Communication activities undertaken during the integration process must be goal directed and measurable. Expectations should be made clear to the employees of the new entity early on in the postmerger integration process.

9. Leadership is an important contributor in the postmerger integration activity.

10. Services of a cross-cultural training consultancy may be used to educate and normalize the employees of the acquired company about the culture of the acquiring company, though significant expenditures for outside expertise do not guarantee a smooth integration.

11. Communication is an important factor for success in a merger, along with other essential elements including functional, financial, and HR integration.

Key Terms

- Culture fit
- Employee buy-in
- Standard procedures
- Integration

Appendix B: A Short Note on Mergers and Acquisitions

It is widely acknowledged that mergers and acquisitions (M&As) enhance economic trade practices. However, laws are essential to regulate dominance, which may be abused. Acquiring firms must be compliant with prevailing competition laws regulating cross border M&As before, during, and after the merger.

Currently the American and European legal systems are the two main models of competition law. The regulations help to ensure that the acquiring firm (through voluntary–mandatory disclosures) preserves a fine balance between ensuring market competitiveness and protecting consumer welfare.

The Sherman Act and Section 7 of the Clayton Act are the primary areas of legislation that address U.S. M&As. The provisions of the Clayton Act are restricted to the territories of the United States. The Sherman Act limits attempts to monopolize or conspiracies to restrain trade or commerce among the states or with foreign nations. The U.S. courts apply U.S. antitrust laws to foreign business activities that involve U.S. entities based on the *effects test*.

Competition law in Europe is concerned more with preventing abuses of dominant market positions than with the dangers that arise out of economic imperialism. European competition law is governed primarily by Articles 85 and 86 of the Treaty Establishing the European Community. Article 85 is similar to the Sherman Act in the U.S. legislation; Article 86 is more concerned with prohibition of abuse of dominant position via unfair trade practices, curtailing production, restrictive pricing, and so on. Another applicable law is the European Community Merger Regulation 139/200449 (ECMR 2004), which has jurisdiction over any activity that has a community dimension. The European Court of Justice (ECJ) has also adopted an approach to extraterritorial enforcement of competition laws similar to that of U.S. courts.

Mergers and Indian Competition Act, 2002

In August 2009, the Monopolies and Restrictive Trade Practices Act, 1969 was repealed and replaced by the Competition Act, 2002, prospectively in effect from 2009 onward. The focus of the new act was on curbing unfair practices rather than on preventing monopolies, which have negative effects on competition both within and outside India. In 2007, the Competition Act was amended to include a mandatory notification process for persons undertaking combinations of business entities above prescribed threshold limits. In 2008, effort was made to provide a framework to regulate combinations, which include M&As of enterprises. Currently, the merger provisions are not in force.

Section 18 of the Competition Act also deals with extraterritorial powers. Regardless of the size of the transaction, notification is required where the combined asset value or turnover in India exceeds a certain value. This means that it is mandatory for a foreign company with assets of more than $500 million that has a subsidiary or joint venture in India with a substantial investment (above $125 million) to notify the Competition Commission before acquiring a company outside India. The company would have to wait for the Competition Commission's approval for a period that could extend to 210 days before the deal could become effective. This waiting period may dissuade foreign investors from investing in India and force them to seek other locations. Currently, Indian corporate and regulatory laws do not permit dual listing, which is preferred by companies to avoid capital gains taxes that result from a merger. It only permits foreign forms to issue Indian Depository Receipts (IDRs), while the Indian firms can issue American Depositary Receipts (ADRs) and Global Depository Receipts (GDRs).

Experts in corporate laws are critical of the regulatory hurdles that a complex merger might encounter in India. They point out the gaps in the Indian corporate laws system pertaining to M&As. High capital controls, political pressures, absence of dual listing, complex takeover code, and partial convertibility of the Indian rupee (the current convertibility rules do not allow an Indian citizen to hold shares in foreign currency, which is different from the cash that such an individual would hold in foreign currency), and the Foreign Exchange Management Act (foreign companies can be listed in India, but only in the form of IDRs and not their underlying shares) are some of the barriers that legal experts recommend should be removed to facilitate cross border mergers and persuade foreign investors to invest in India.

CHAPTER 7

Implementation, Problem Solving, and Decision Making in Cultures

Despite apparent differences in complexity of decision problems across cultures, the core issues are essentially the same—fulfillment of human needs, protection of the individual, promoting group survival, and maintenance of community norms and standards

—Mann et al. (1998, p 326)

Introduction

Decision making is fundamental to the job of a manager. Socialization and differing business environments, however, can influence both the decision-making process and the choices. With significant growth in international interactions, it is now more important than ever to understand how people from different nationalities make decisions. Top management team (TMT) member orientation and decision-making style is generally not consistent across national boundaries. Values and beliefs, as they are characterized by national culture, have the potential to influence managerial decision making. Managers now need to know not only about the culture of the person they are interacting with but also about their personality, behavior, communication styles in conflict situations, demographics, and lifestyles.

Not only corporate giants but middle-sized companies are also going global to achieve economies of scale. Managers must not only make strategic choices but also restructure organizations, functions, and processes. Flatter organization structures have led to the growth of globally scattered matrix teams. Today's cross-cultural teams have to work cross functionally as well as cross-culturally. In the current scenario, teams—marketing, virtual, research and development, production, and product development—are essentially cross-cultural in nature. Team members represent different cultures, each with their unique set of behavioral norms and ability to create, transmit, store, process, and transfer internally defined critical information.

Cross-Cultural Work Group

A cross-cultural work group or team comprises members belonging to different geographic, ethnic, and national boundaries. Team members differ from one another with respect to cultural, mental, and social programming. Groups may be defined in terms of cross-cultural work groups and multinational teams and task groups and may be formal or informal, localized or dispersed, and of short-term or long-term appointment.

A typical scenario at the workplace

While interacting in a cross-cultural group work, group members of a typical cross-cultural team initially encountered problems relating to language. Members spoke in Japanese, Korean, French, and German. Though translators were utilized, the process took time and proved costly. Then the group resolved to use English as the language of group communication. This created a fresh set of problems. The Japanese could hardly communicate in English, and the Germans' English was rough and heavily accented. The French were not keen on speaking English at all. The Koreans were aggressive and resisted participation in the conversations. The working of the team was problematic because the group could not sacrifice national preferences for international commitment. However, the group acknowledged that conflicting styles were creating obstacles and that there was a greater need for cooperation. Finally, an international consultant was called to help the group create synergy among themselves.

Team Development in a Cross-Cultural Work Group

There is a growing realization that individual technical brilliance is no longer the only requisite for effective work performance in independent team assignments. Cross-cultural synergy needs to be realized to bring about desired results.

Team development in a cross-cultural work group essentially takes place in four stages (see Figure 7.1 in the following text).

Configure

The first stage is the group constitution stage. Members come together for the first time and examine, through their particular cultural lenses, the composition of the team and task requirements. The stage can include culture shock, language problems, and ambiguity. Members realize that they are different from each other in terms of nationality and culture. The members, through their particular cultural lens, examine the fit between the members' culture of origin culture of residence and the task at hand.

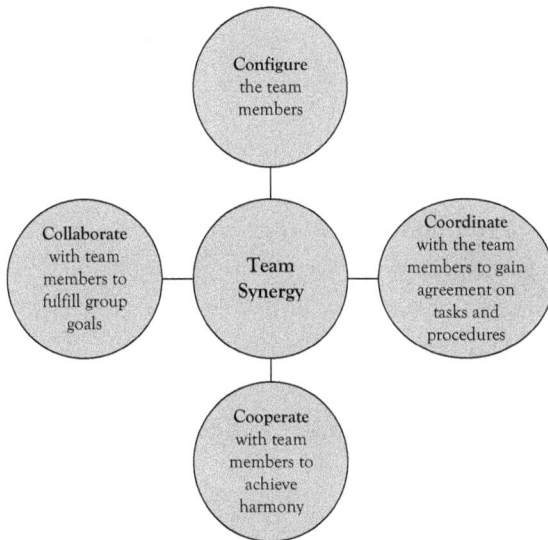

Figure 7.1 Stages in multicultural team development

Coordinate

The second phase involves gaining agreement on tasks and procedures. Task allocation is determined, taking into consideration the members' complementary and universal skills. Members agree on best times to schedules meetings, language of instruction, frequency and mode of interaction, decision-making roles and responsibilities, hierarchy, leadership issues, prioritizing of short-term and long-term plans, and behavioral norms.

Cooperate

The third phase involves building rapport among team members through the exercise of effective interpersonal skills. Barriers to communication include dominance by an individual or a major subgroup, deliberate politeness, and exclusion of certain members. Research reveals that members often adapt their behaviors, behaving not only as they would in their home culture but in the other cultures of the work group also. Crucial outcomes of this phase include trust, cooperation, and communication. Ethnocentric attitudes are explored so that disruptions and misunderstandings are minimized. Teams are quite susceptible to breakup at this juncture.

Collaborate

The fourth phase is reached when the work group begins to function like a work team. The hallmark of this stage is risk-free (no member feels discriminated against) communication. Synergy (group output is more than individual output) replaces groupthink (tendency of individual group members to align their views with the group leader), and the team is focused on task completion.

The following communication variables can impact the level of collaboration achieved:

- Frequency of communication among group members
- Existence of a common language of communication
- Frequency of exchange of task-related information

- Manner in which conflicts are resolved
- Demonstration of positive nonverbal behaviors
- Degree of engagement in informal conversation
- Effectiveness of persuasion and reasoning among members
- Methods of communication

Tapas Mohapatra, Implementation Coach at McKinsey & Company, Mumbai

When communicating with others, I focus on the "richness" of my idea. I prepare the content thoroughly so that I come across as prepared. It is important for me to pay respect to people belonging to a culture different from mine. This is evident in the small gestures that I make when I am conversing with them.

It has been noted that diversity creates greater bottlenecks in intraorganization and domestic cultures than in multicultural teams. Employees belonging to the same cultures are often reluctant to recognize internal conflicts within an organization. For instance, there is greater synergy between English-speaking Americans and Canadians than between Anglophone and Francophone Canadians.

Norms of Decision Making in Eastern and Western Societies

There are stark differences between Eastern and Western cultures as to who makes the decision, who is consulted, who gives inputs, and even bases on which decisions that are made. For example, the Western way of decision making has been described as objective, rational, and impersonal, in contrast to the Eastern way of deciding, which is subjective, emotional, and personal. There has also been a strong debate with respect to the positive and negative effects of TMT, demographic heterogeneity on intervening processes, as well as team processes. At one end, assertions have been made that TMT heterogeneity paves the way for an enhanced level of brainstorming, variety of strategies, problem-solving methods, and consequently, better decision making. On the other hand, management scholars contend that heterogeneous teams take too much time to resolve contentious interpersonal issues for the team to focus much on effective decision making. Recent studies have examined the impact of various demographic variables on TMT effectiveness, including TMT tenure, educational background, functional background, and impact on corporate profitability (Grecke and House 2012).

Literature on cross-cultural communication reveals that typically people from all cultures tend to be overconfident in life and those from the Eastern societies even more so. While some cultures are perceived to be more risk averse than others (Western societies), there are other cultures that embrace risk as a way of life (some Asian countries). Some cultures value decision making by consensus (Swedes, Japanese), while others prefer to avoid the use of groupthink altogether. Barriers also arise when fatalistic cultures feel uncomfortable planning for the long term.

A study exploring the attitudes of German and Indian students toward strategic aspects of problem solving found that Germans were more vocal and control oriented and committed fewer errors than the Indian students. The Germans were accustomed to making decisions themselves, unlike the Indian students who relied on others' support to arrive at a decision. Similar results were found in studies examining differences in decision-making and problem-solving processes (weighing alternatives, accepting trade-offs, information choices, etc.) and the use of audiovisual aids among different cultures. The study is not clear as to which employees were more productive—the Germans or the Indians.

Even cultures in the same geographic zones often differ from each other in their problem-solving and decision-making processes. The Cartesian model, (derived from the French philosopher Descartes), is the basis for French rationalism and the inductive logic that guides French decision making. As a result, the French tend to consider all aspects before arriving at a decision. However, their actions tend to be more subjective and less concrete. They like to explore various options and do not mind having multiple meetings to finalize a market strategy or business decision. They like to demonstrate their intellect by customizing customer solutions.

French managers like to present individualistic ideas to demonstrate their intellectual capacity. Decision making is made by the heads of departments, while the middle and the lower managers administer the decisions. Thus, decisions are usually implemented by those who had no say in the original decision making. French control is also tight at various levels to compensate for low levels of commitment from the implementers.

The Danish on the other hand are methodological, pragmatic, and less engaged in their approach to decision making; when they make a report, it is less emotional and more down to earth. They speak in a clear-cut manner and are decisive in their thought process. They usually prefer short meetings to decide strategic issues. The decision makers are usually the implementers, and therefore their commitment level is higher. Control is less tight among the Danes due in part to the concept of responsible autonomy. The Danes gauge effectiveness by teamwork and cooperation as well as the output obtained, than a mere demonstration of their superior intelligence. Actionable goals and realistic implementation plans are strongly emphasized, rather than intellectual debate and argumentative discussion.

In China, the strong influence of the local as well as regional government is evident in the decision-making process. Organizations such as the Ministry of Commerce, People's Bank of China, State Administration of Taxation, China Banking Regulatory Commission, and State-Owned Assets Supervision and Administration Commission (SASAC) are extremely important to foreign investors in operational and financial matters. Experts recommend that investors must exercise patience and diplomacy in their dealings with these agencies especially when seeking permits or approvals.

Japanese problem-solving methods involve the use of *jidoka*—a method by which problems are resolved as soon as they arise through detailed analysis and discussion so that they do not recur. Continuous improvement or *kaizen* eliminates anything that is a variation of the standard. Decisions are rarely made at Japanese meetings. Meetings are held either to convey information or to convey a decision already made by the senior management. The idea of *nemawashi* (roots of a tree) implies that discussions and debates are to take place before the meeting actually takes place. Implicit to this idea are the concepts of *honne* and *tatamae* where what one publicly states (*tatamae*) is often vastly different from what one personally thinks (*honne*). Decisions are reached through the process of consensus building and is concerned with the preservation of *wa* (group harmony).

> In a decision-making situation, an American manager described that the Japanese took days and sometimes weeks to arrive at a decision. The strong need of the Japanese for affiliation was paramount for preserving old relationships and cultivating new ones. Reaching a consensus was a painfully slow process; however, they made up for it by speeding up the implementation. The manager found that in comparison, the Chinese were quicker in deciding, but lacked implementation effectiveness. They liked to exercise power and control to influence the direction of decision making. The Americans were analyzers who analyzed situations and identified possible solutions through a structured decision-making process. Thus, the Americans could work around the prevailing power structure to enforce decision making, unlike the Chinese and the Japanese who are careful not to disturb the prevailing power structure.

India is a hierarchical society, and positional power is thus considered valuable. Organizational roles are strictly defined, with the attitude of the superior often paternalistic toward the employees. Managers ensure that they know about the family and health aspects of their employees apart from purely professional contexts. Indians do not generally react positively to criticism and tend to withdraw from group meetings when confronted with it. The culture is relationship as well as group oriented; therefore, preserving harmony is important. In terms of decision making, managers and subordinates feel comfortable consulting with each other during important decision-making meetings. Indians are also not averse to risk-taking in business decision making. Decisions are mostly made on the basis of the collective good of those impacted by the decision rather than on the strength of sheer numbers and percentages.

To conclude, cross-cultural group workings involve the intensive use of information and communication technologies, especially for virtual teams that have few if any opportunities for face-to-face interaction. The challenge before multicultural executive teams is twofold. First, they must develop a situational analysis of the business problems confronting the organization and involve the various members in expressing their ideas about desirable solutions, and arrange and rearrange the information for best results. The second challenge would be to quickly resolve differences among team members and spend the team's valuable time and energy on problem solving. The cultural intelligence of the manager is critical to both processes.

Summary

1. Flatter organization structures have led to the growth of matrix teams scattered globally.
2. In current business environments, teams of all types are essentially cross-cultural in nature.
3. Decision making is fundamental to the job of a manager. However, socialization and differing business environments influence both the decision-making process and the choices that managers make.
4. There is a stark difference between Eastern and Western cultures on certain aspects of decision making, such as who makes the decision, who is consulted, decisions and solving problems, and the values and interests.
5. Even cultures in the same geographic zones often differ from each other in their problem-solving and decision-making processes.
6. Managers now need to know not only about the culture of the person they are interacting with, but also about their personality, behavior, communication styles in conflict situations, demographics, and lifestyle.
7. Team development in a cross-cultural work group essentially takes place in four stages—configure, coordinate, cooperate, and collaborate.
8. The challenge before multicultural executive teams is twofold: one, to develop a situational analysis of the business problem confronting the organization and two, to efficiently resolve differences among

themselves and spend time on problem solving. The level of cultural intelligence of the manager is essential to these processes.

Key Terms

- Socialization
- Diversity
- TMT

CHAPTER 8

Communication Skills in International Business Negotiations

He, who knows his enemy and himself well, will not be defeated easily
—Sun Tzu, Art of War

Introduction

The word *negotiation* stems from the Roman word *negotiari*, which means *to carry on business* and is derived from the Latin root words *neg* (not) and *otium* (ease and leisure). It is thus, a business activity, which demands strategic planning and hectic parleys. Achieving success in business negotiations is one of the most challenging communicative tasks in business.

Broadly speaking, negotiation between two or more parties involves the process of communicating back and forth to arrive at a mutually satisfying agreement. It is thus, a kind of social interaction, which facilitates cooperation over conflict (of interests), agreement over disagreement, and collaboration over competition.

A typical cross border negotiation process occurs in five stages (see Figure 8.1). These may be divided into non-task related and task-related activities. The first stage is nontask related and involves rapport building with the negotiating party. This is followed by hard and soft bargaining strategies, which are task-related activities. The deal is concluded with a show of hospitality toward the visiting party.

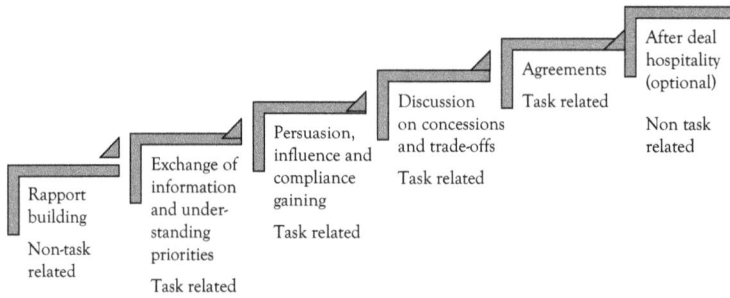

Figure 8.1 Stages in cross border negotiations

Culture and Negotiation

Different cultures practice different negotiation styles. These styles originate from differences in communication, persuasion and influencing styles, differences in societal structures (hierarchical or egalitarian), group norms, gender roles, protocols, education systems, religious inclinations, cultural norms, and traditions. Indeed, the cause of unsuccessful negotiations is often due to differences in cultures rather than political, economic, or legal issues.

Cultural differences impact international business negotiations significantly. In cross border or international negotiations, failure to account for these differences can adversely affect entry strategy decisions such as selection of target country markets, product launches in target countries, and implementation of operational and marketing programs.

Western negotiators often face a challenge with Chinese counterparts mainly on account of differences in cultures. Chinese can be tough negotiators as well as warm hosts simultaneously and place a large premium on communication and hospitality. Coupled with complicated business rituals and social etiquette and heavy reliance on interpersonal relationship building, the process can get long drawn and strained. Western negotiators may view the Chinese with suspicion and distrust due to their indirectness; the Chinese on the other hand brand Westerners as aggressive, insincere, and too impersonal due to their directness.

Negotiation is essentially an attempt to extract information about the other party as well as gather information from the other party. Each party is interested in knowing about the other's interest in the proposal and the motives for their positions. This exchange paves the way for integrative negotiation. However, the process of information gathering is tricky. This is because negotiation is often a game of perception and projection.

Convergent Communication Skills and the Expert Negotiator

Integrative negotiation requires convergent communication skills. Negotiators must have the ability to identify not only their own interests but also those of the opponents. Negotiators should also be able to appreciate the opponent's as well their own priorities. This should lead to beneficial trade-offs and mutually satisfying options, which are the heart of an integrative negotiation solution. Negotiators can opt for a systematic questioning approach to understand the interests and priorities of opponents. Conversely, they can adopt a trial and error approach to judge the interests and priorities of the other. Every society places a different degree of importance on relationship development, decision making, contract arrangements, and debatable activities such as bribing. An effective negotiator understands these variables and communicates accordingly. Experts recommend that the ideal negotiator should move away from stereotyping (Chinese are tough negotiators, Arabs welcome interruptions, Americans are direct, Germans are time bound) and labeling (task focused; people focused) and focus on individuals since deals are conducted by individuals (Figure 8.2).

Communication skills of the expert negotiator				
Restrained facial expression and body language	Listening skills—to understand cues, clues, signs, and signals	Conflict management skills—knowing when to argue and when to accommodate	Articulate—can converse knowledgeably on legal and government regulations	Flexible—can adapt to people and situations

Figure 8.2 Fluency and articulation flexibility

An American keen to do business with a Japanese firm

I was both confused and perplexed. Here was this Japanese negotiator who was born in Tokyo, educated at Wharton, worked in Chicago … frankly I did not have a strategy to deal with him. He appeared to be one of us. His style of talking, decision making, and problem solving was so unlike the stereotype of Japanese that I had come prepared to deal with.

Generalizations, however, form the focal point or the mean metric by which a culture may be judged (see Table 8.1 in the following text). Therefore, generalizations may be taken as a basis for seeking an understanding of the people of a different culture.

Table 8.1 Communication in negotiations—helpful generalizations about Asian and Western cultures

S. no.	Western style	Asian style
1	Direct, low-context communication	Indirect, high-context communication
2	Efficient information exchange	Repetitive questions
3	Time pressure	Unlimited time
4	Individual	Collective
5	Individual decision maker; team with authority	Group decision makers; team without authority
6	Early task focus; get down to business	Early nontask focus; banquets and sightseeing
7	Contract	Relationship
8	A contract is a contract	Renegotiation is always possible
9	Long, detailed contracts	Short, general contracts
10	Contingencies predetermined in the contract	Contingencies settled by friendly negotiations
11	Short-term focus	Long-term focus
12	Issue-by-issue negotiation agenda	All issues always open to negotiation
13	Profits focus	Market share, future focus
14	Limited government involvement in deal-making	Significant government involvement in deal-making
15	Business	Friendship

Standard Preparatory Assessments for Cross Border Negotiations

Culture influences the negotiation processes in many ways. The most obvious is the way each culture views the process itself. For example, the Americans view negotiation as a competitive process, the Japanese as an information-sharing process, and the Russians as a winning proposition. This decides the tenor of the communication. For instance, logic and precision guide most Westerners, and they find it difficult to accept arguments based on compromise rather than a rational thought process. This backdrop likely prompted President Sarkozy's comment at a recent G20 summit: "I prefer a clash to a flabby consensus."

Communication strategies during a negotiation

Communication strategies during a negotiation involve consideration of the following variables (also see Appendix C at the end of the chapter):

- How much time is usually spent in negotiating?
- How many team members are expected?
- What levels do they represent?
- What is the level of socializing one is expected to do?
- How many interruptions can be expected during the negotiation processes?
- What is the level of formality? Does one need to use titles to address people?
- Does one need to be direct or indirect in communication?
- What is the attitude toward gender?
- Is persuasion fact based or emotion based?
- Do the negotiators show their emotions and feelings or hide their feelings?
- What is the propensity to deal with uncertainties and surprises during a negotiation?
- Are arguments built from general to specific or specific to general?
- Is the contract a starting point or the end of the negotiation?

Experiences of a negotiator

As a group we felt isolated by the Chinese deal makers. They looked stern and uncompromising. Their faces revealed nothing.... They looked at each and every point in the records to confirm or validate what we had been saying and pointed out inconsistencies at frequent intervals. At the same time they were keen to make us feel comfortable in China...treating us to lavish dinners and taking us for sightseeing!

The Japanese will say "yes" intermittently; however yes in their culture is anything but a sign of agreement...They will suddenly leave the discussion and huddle in groups. They can be very strategic and manipulative in their intent.

The Russians are hard bargainers and will try their best to keep the price low. They can be dramatic and persistent in their talk tactics and make pretense of leaving the table if the terms and conditions are not met. Russians take negotiations very seriously. The informal tone of US—American business partners for example—is often not serious enough for their liking. When negotiating with Russians, one should be punctual and, decide on binding goals, and comply with them. Personal connections are therefore very helpful. Generally, one must be prepared to be met with a healthy portion of suspicion. Russians favor accuracy in contracts. In Russia political discussions should best be avoided. Russians, however, are well read and well versed in literature, arts, and culture.

The Americans like to keep it light and humorous.

The British are quite like the Americans, only a bit more formal.

The Arabs can be stubborn and rigid. They can stall a discussion if "Allah" does not approve.

The Mexicans, Italians, Spanish, Brazilians, Turks, French, Koreans, and the Indians express very verbally.

The Germans, Japanese, and the Dutch are not voluble at all.

Another important aspect of the negotiation process is the selection of the negotiators. Cultures vary in their criteria for choosing personnel for an international negotiation. For some it could be age; for others, it could be knowledge, rank, seniority, gender, or experience. Cultures also dictate protocol, norms of communication, and the nature of the agreements.

Some studies support that South African negotiators are more tolerant of other cultures mainly because of their experiences of living in a culturally diverse country, their belief in the philosophy of *ubuntu* (self-identity though group), and their exposure to processes relating to political transformation, reconciliation, and nation building (Woo and Prud'homme 1999).

Etiquette, Protocol, and Behavior

Negotiators need knowledge about local customs and taboos, greetings, gift giving, use of silence, exchange of business cards, time management in meetings and presentations, use of space, eye contact, table manners, dressing style, and general deportment. The use of numbers is another cultural variable, as shown in Table 8.2 in the following text:

Cultural Intelligence

Individual versus collectivist orientation, nature of relationships, high-context or low-context orientation, approach toward time management, use of personal space, egalitarianism or hierarchical view, and degree of risk-taking are some of the cultural factors to be taken into account in negotiation. One important fallacy is that national culture is the most distinctive indicator of cultural factors of a nation. Though each country has

Table 8.2 Use of numbers in different cultures

S. no.	Arabic numeral	Countries
1	Number 3	Valued by Taiwan, Monaco; not valued by Europe
2	Number 4	Disliked by the Chinese, Taiwanese, and Japanese
3	Number 6	Liked by Southeast Asians
4	Number 7	Liked by those practicing Islam; negative number in Singapore
5	Number 8	Liked by the Chinese
6	Number 13	Disliked by Westerners

Shashank Sinha, President, International Business, Godrej Consumer Products Ltd.

"I have travelled to many places such as Shanghai, South Asia, Argentina, Brazil, Africa and London for business deals and transactions. To be successful internationally, I feel that one must have a positive attitude toward ambiguity coupled with a strong sense of curiosity."

a distinct national culture, there are variations within every nation. Some examples are that of the United States (which itself is a blend of many cultures) and India (again, a nation of many subcultures and subgroups).

Team communication, problem solving, and decision making

Understanding ways in which deal-making groups communicate is crucial in influencing key members. This also includes forms of information sharing and the governance process of decision making. Other factors include decision-making rights, authoritarian versus empowerment leadership, consensus or hierarchical decision making, formal or informal relationships, and main group or subgroup focus. Differences exist even in similar cultures and subgroups as Figure 8.3 reveals in the following text (Chang 2011).

Economic and political climate considerations

These include awareness of laws and government policies related to the type of arrangement being sought, such as a joint venture, merger, acquisition, or simple partnership. It is also important to appreciate the

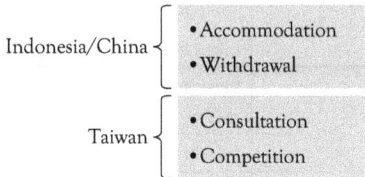

Figure 8.3 Differences exist even in similar cultures and subgroups

political ethos related to cross border investments: Does the government favor state control or privatization?

The negotiation-specific category assessments include the following:

- The opponents and their interests.
- Their no-deal options.
- Opportunities to claim value.
- Opportunities to create value.
- The most promising sequence.
- The process design: For instance, while negotiating with the Arabs, it is important to know that the decision making is centralized. It is controlled by the government, the members of the House of Saud, and the commercial elite. The process then has to be designed with these parameters in mind.
- Possible objections.
- Possible concessions.

Role of Language in Negotiation

In intercultural negotiation, unless the two countries have the same mother tongue, English is frequently adopted as the preferred medium of communication. If this is not possible, the services of translators or interpreters are used to assist the teams in communicating with each other. In negotiation situations, it is important to fully comprehend both the literal meaning (surface meaning) as well as the symbolic meaning of language.

Muzukashii (Japanese) means difficult in English (literal meaning) or a hard bargain (American). Muzukashii for the Japanese means out of question. While difficult implies that there is still some possibility, out of question negates the very possibility.

The Japanese also have different ways of saying no and one must understand the context to appreciate the symbolic meaning of each type of no. A silence could also be a no, as could leaving the room suddenly, raising a counter question, lying, delaying a response, refusing to answer a question, and using "but" after yes, among others (see Appendix C for insight on culture and negotiation styles).

Summary

1. Achieving success in negotiations is one of the most challenging communicative tasks in business.
2. Different cultures practice different negotiation styles. These originate from differences in communication, persuasion, and influencing styles, differences in societal structures (hierarchical or egalitarian), group norms, gender roles, protocols, education systems, religious inclinations, cultural norms, and traditions.
3. Integrative negotiation requires convergent communication skills. Negotiators must have the ability to identify not only their own interests but also those of the opponents.
4. Experts recommend that the ideal negotiator should move away from stereotyping and focus on individuals since deals are conducted by individuals.
5. There are two categories of standard preparatory assessments for cross border negotiations—the general category assessments and the negotiation-specific category assessments.
6. In a negotiation, it is important to fully comprehend both the literal meaning (surface meaning) as well as the symbolic meaning of language.

Key Terms

- Convergent communication skills
- Cultural intelligence

Appendix C: Negotiation Styles and Culture

Goodwill and relationship building

Goodwill and positive relations count a lot in Saudi Arabian culture. Social cliques can block a proposal. Saudis believe in hospitality. An agent or a middleman is important to reach out for the right connections and develop contacts. China, Taiwan and Thailand believe in importance of middleman or an agent; believe in hospality to 'disarm' the opponent.

Criteria for selection of the term of negotiators

In Saudi Arabia, seniority and age; in the US and Germans, knowledge and expertise, In china, position and hierarchy, In Japan, seniority and position

Type of presentation

Visual presentation in Saudi Arabia; visual presentation, along with prototype of the product; in the US, replace with facts, evidence and statistics. German more focused on features and design than pricing

Communication

Saudis are not confrontational; they may use delaying and hedging tactics to avoid saying a direct 'no'. They do not people to be haughty and arrogance puts them off. They also do not like if people are in a hurry to do business. They invest a lot of the initial time on relationship building. Hospitality, and getting acquainted with the group.

Follow up and implementation

The Saudi government likes to use the turnkey approach in huge construction projects. Saudis respond to close and constant personal follow up - not to mere correspondence or long-distance phone calls. Germans like to keep in touch via detailed emails.

Gender

In Saudi Arabia, women must desist from negotiating with Saudi officials, as the men in this county are hesitant to deal with women. In japan, women negotiators are few and far between.

Interruptions

Quite frequent in Saudi Arabia, perceived as a sign from 'Allan' to think carefully about the deal: They still observe the traditional 'majlis' system and the 'diwaniyan' culture of meeting people in their offices or homes to resolve personal as well as professional issues. Not at all in US; less frequent but occurs I Japan and China. Koreans interrupt others while talking more than any other Asian nation.

Signing of Contracts

Saudis have a greater preference for the oral word over the written contract although they may take pains to draft it. Parties need to be very specific about the contract details since it is usually very difficult to dispute it in Saudi Arabia. All written materials must be in English as well as in Arabic. *Chinese tend to renegotiate the contractual agreement. This is because unlike the Americans Chinese view the contractual agreement. This is because unlike the Americans Chinese view the contract as the first concrete signal of the commitment of the parties for a long term relationship. For them the contract is a beginning rather the end of discussions. Changes are made intermittently, in an unstructured fashion; issues are dealt with as they arise. Russians are also very formal about contracts signing and stamps.*

Source: Adapted from LeBaron (July, 2003).

CHAPTER 9

The Etiquette Advantage in Global Business

Good manners can open doors that the best education cannot
—Clarence Thomas

Introduction

Worldwide, there is an increased pressure to differentiate the quality of products and services. How a business projects itself internationally is more important than ever before. A company's employees are the major carriers of the image of the company and the culture they represent. This action assumes greater importance when doing business with other cultures. Whether one is engaged in price negotiations, delivering a presentation, attending a trade fair, or applying to a company for a job, appropriate business etiquette helps to build rapport, foster trust, and reduce misunderstandings.

Etiquette is described as socially acceptable customs and behaviors. Breaking these codes is not considered a crime in the legal sense of the term; however, it may invite censure or contempt. It is expected in business that such rules are observed on occasions such as negotiations, presentations, and meetings, and in the writing of e-mail messages and letters.

Etiquette is grounded in manners. Most children learn early in life to be polite and courteous. While people imbibe manners in early childhood, etiquette has to be learned. You must learn, for example, which cutlery is used for wine and what dress to wear for a particular occasion. To be successful in international business activity, you must understand cultural differences in etiquette, preferences and expectations, and the contexts in which these are applicable.

The global head of human resources of one of the world's leading information technology services companies, Nandita Gurjar, agrees that cultural awareness and cross border ambitions are tied together. In an interview, she reiterated that for a global company, cultural know-how is absolutely essential.

Source: The Economist Intelligence Unit (2012).

Misunderstandings are usually rooted in cultural differences, and these threaten to destabilize cross border collaborations. Figure 9.1 summarizes key points of etiquette.

As with all aspects relating to culture, one has to be mindful of the difference between generalizations and stereotypes relating to etiquette expectations. For example, the concept of relationship building or *guanxi* is emphasized as appropriate in the Chinese context. Visitors and expatriates believe that one way to build this with the Chinese is to give them gifts. They are advised that they should avoid giving clocks, straw sandals, handkerchiefs, or items depicting a stork or a crane. They tend to interpret this either too narrowly (giving gifts perfunctorily, without any real relationship building) or too broadly (expensive wining and dining along with elaborate gifting for days). Recent reports suggest that the Chinese are moving away from elaborate gift-giving rituals and focusing

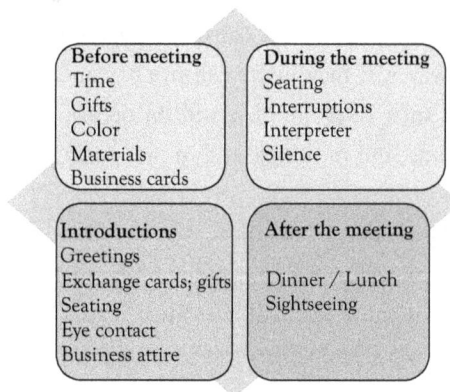

Before meeting	During the meeting
Time	Seating
Gifts	Interruptions
Color	Interpreter
Materials	Silence
Business cards	

Introductions	After the meeting
Greetings	
Exchange cards; gifts	Dinner / Lunch
Seating	Sightseeing
Eye contact	
Business attire	

Figure 9.1 Areas of misunderstanding in cross-cultural communication

on the value that a potential business partner might bring to the table (The Economist Intelligence Unit, 2012).

Important Points of Etiquette

The following points of etiquette are generally recognized as important when visiting other countries:

Greetings

Cultures differ in their types of greetings, as shown in Figure 9.2. Americans prefer the handshake in formal settings; the French kiss the cheek; the Arabs use the traditional Bedouin greeting (kiss on both the cheeks and a hug); the Japanese prefer the bow (the deeper it is, the more respectful); Indians do the *namaskar* (both palms are folded, accompanied with a short bow). Light handshakes are acceptable in China, and the Chinese should initiate the action. Bowing with the palms together is common. The French are particular about introductions, and

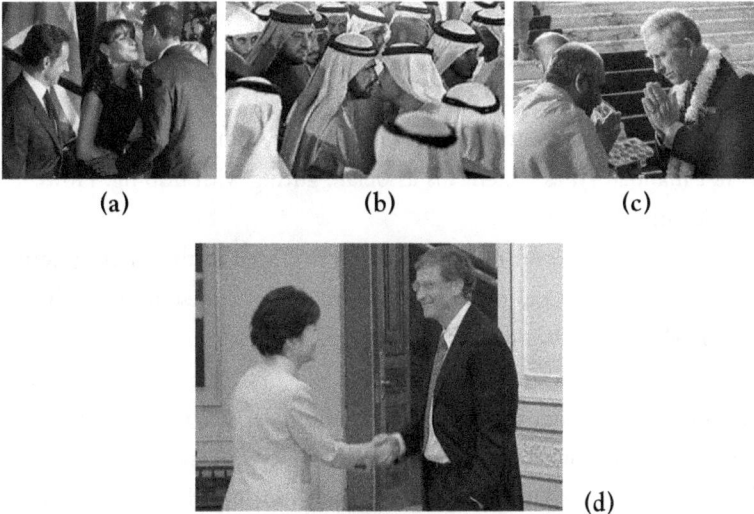

(a)   (b)   (c)

(d)

Figure 9.2 Differing greeting customs: (a) the French way to greet, (b) the traditional Arab way to greet each other, (c) the Indian way to greet, (d) a disrespectful handshake? Bill Gates, Microsoft, greeting the South Korean leader

these are usually conducted by the third party. While handshakes are most common in business, travelers would be wise to know the cultural preferences in greetings in different regions of the world.

South Korea is a hierarchical culture where etiquette is valued highly. In the accompanying photo, Bill Gates is seen shaking hands with the South Korean President Park Geun-hye in a manner perceived as too casual by many South Koreans. "Cultural difference, or an act of disrespect?" the *Joong Ang Ilbo* newspaper wrote in the accompanying caption. What Gates may not have realized is that in some Asian countries, a handshake is only done with friends or casual acquaintances. It is considered rude to shake hands with one hand in the pocket. Chung Jin-suk, secretary general at the Korean National Assembly was quoted in the Korean news press as stating that Gates' all-American style was rather casual. Several questions were raised in the social media sites: Was Bill Gates trying to dominate the South Koreans by this act? Was he trying to get the upper edge? (AFP 2013).

Business Cards and Giving Gifts

In the United States, business card exchange is considered a formality and a way to promote business. Cards should be neat, clean, and legible. They should be passed out before the beginning of a meeting. In the United States, it is not taboo to write anything on a business card. Giving gifts is not mandatory, as Americans associate gifting with bribing. However, ethnic gifts may be given.

The Chinese expect to be formally introduced to the guest by someone else. Usually, titles are used to address the Chinese hosts (Manager Lee or Mr. Lee). Chinese view business cards as a way to develop relationships. The Chinese card exchange is formal, and the norm is that one side of the card contains English, while the other side of the card has the Chinese translation of the credentials. They give and take cards with both hands. Among the Chinese, gifts are freely exchanged in business deals. The senior most person gets the gift first, followed by the next person in the hierarchy. Chinese do not like gifts to be opened in front of them. When exchanging gifts, they are sensitive to the color of the wrapping, the type of gift, and the price tag of the gift. Black, blue, and white are colors that signify death and are best avoided. They also have an aversion to the number 4.

Dining

The traditional Indian food is rich, aromatic, spicy, and variegated. Indians also serve continental, Italian, Chinese, Lebanese, and other cuisines. Visitors must sample all the dishes and praise the food. Indians eat bread with their hands and are not avid users of the fork and knife. Lunch and dinner are occasions to discuss business matters. Alcoholic beverages are usually avoided in business lunches or dinners. Time is valued, but late coming is acceptable. In Japan, it is important to be prompt for social and business events. Japanese do not address people by their first names in business. Usually, the person is addressed by the last name with the title *san* added to it (Mr. Lun-San). Japanese do not usually bring their spouses to business occasions; it is wise to ask Japanese men if they are bringing their wives along for an event. Though times are changing, Japanese men are not yet quite accustomed to interacting with women managers. Soup may be eaten directly from the bowl without a "utensil". Chopsticks are usually used for eating fish and rice, though outsiders may ask for forks as well. Sauces are not poured over the food; rather these are used as dips. After the meal, the forks are not to be placed upright; they are to be placed alongside the plate or the bowl. Chopsticks must not be used to point at something. They must also not be licked. The Japanese prefer

The typical Indian food plate also called thali

that their drinks be refilled by the guest, and in turn they would refill the guests' glasses.

In China, business dinners start early at around 6 p.m. or so, and are ritualistic events. Guests are seated opposite the host (head) if the table is rectangular; otherwise, by his side. The host is seated farthest from the door, and seating is hierarchical. This is done to regulate conversations between the same levels. The Chinese napkin is small and not kept on the lap; it is used for many purposes. Toasting is done regularly after a drink; usually the toast is first raised to the most senior person. It is a good idea to serve drinks to others as well. Guests should be able to use chopsticks to eat rice and other foods. Chopsticks in China are round as compared to those of the Japanese, which are rectangular shaped. Visitors are usually advised to observe the host and then emulate their actions to avoid embarrassment. Tipping is best avoided in China. It is a good idea to praise the host for his or her preparation or choice of ordering of the food. Participation in after-dinner entertainment builds relationships with the Chinese.

Tapas Mohapatra, Implementation Coach at McKinsey & Company, Mumbai

"Consider dinners and post-meeting engagements as an exercise in rapport building...it would be wise to check the menu beforehand if you are a vegetarian or have specific food preferences... in case you do want to skip the dinner, excuse yourself by voicing a health concern rather than saying that you have 'work to do' or that 'you are busy.' Koreans are somewhat different from other Asians in that they tend to be more aggressive and boisterous. They show more abandon in their drinking styles and expect visitors to join in. Drinking in Korea is a ritualistic event and perceived as useful to build relationships and strong bonds.

Germans also do not like to discuss business over food. Alcoholic beverages are served and drinks are initiated by the host who raises a toast to the lady by his side. The continental style of the fork and knife is used. After the business dinner is over, the cutlery is placed in the 5.20 position. Germans are quite particular about promptness.

In a recently concluded Commonwealth meeting of foreign ministers, Baird, the direct-talking foreign affairs minister of Canada, found himself in troubled waters over his alleged inappropriate and derogatory remarks to Maldives officials. The minister voiced concerns about the delay of the Maldives' runoff election and reports of violence and intimidation, which are internal and private concerns of Maldives.

Source: The Canadian Press (October 2013).

The Americans have their own unique style of using the fork and knife. The food is cut with the knife in the right hand and the fork held in the left, followed by switching of the hands to eat with the fork in the right hand. Soups and liquids are consumed outside in. Bags are placed on the floor (not on the table) and the napkin on the lap. Business conversations commonly take place during business lunches and dinners. The person who has called for the meeting will typically pay the bill. Tipping is expected in the American dining setup. Like the Germans, Americans are also particular about promptness.

In Mexico, it is quite normal for guests to arrive 20 to 30 minutes late to dinner. Most aspects of etiquette are similar to those of the United States; however, in Mexico, hands are kept on the table throughout the meal. Tipping is prevalent in Mexico.

Small Talk

It is also important in business etiquette to know about what to talk about in international gatherings. For instance, in China, it is wise to refrain from mentioning Tibet, Taiwan, and Tiananmen as these are sensitive issues for the Chinese. The 1947 Partition, similarly, is a sensitive issue both in India and Pakistan.

Summary

1. Standards of conduct are heavily rooted in culture and heritage and vary from country to country.

2. Whether one is engaged in price negotiations, delivering a presentation, attending a trade fair, or applying to a company for a job, appropriate business etiquette helps to build rapport, foster trust, and reduce misunderstandings.

3. One can be assured of international business success if one is prepared for it.

4. The following aspects of etiquette are universally recognized as important when visiting countries: greetings, use of business cards, gift giving, and business dining etiquette.

5. Careful observance of the social customs of an international host will go far in bridging the cultural divide.

Key Terms

- Image carriers
- Small talk
- Punctuality
- Appropriate gifts

CHAPTER 10

Indian Business Culture and Communication

India is the cradle of the human race, the birthplace of human speech, the mother of history, the grandmother of legend, and the great grand-mother of tradition...

—Mark Twain

Introduction

The name *India* is derived from the river Indus, which was home to one of the earliest civilizations of the world. India comprises roughly 17 percent of the world's population with a population density of 324 persons per square kilometer. At the last count, there were 933 females for every 1,000 males. Literacy rate is around 65 percent, with more literate males than females.

The Wonder That Is India

India is credited with a number of firsts, including the invention of chess and the development of mathematical concepts related to algebra, trigonometry, calculus, the place value system, and the decimal system. The earliest school of medicine—*Ayurveda*—was developed in India. An Indian scientist Bhaskaracharya calculated the approximate time it would take the earth to orbit the sun at 365.258756484 days in his treatise, *Surya Siddhant*. The value of pi was calculated by an Indian mathematician, Budhayana who also explained the concept of the Pythagorean theorem in the sixth century. India currently exports software to over 90 countries. A multilingual, multiethnic, multiracial, and multicaste society, India is the birthplace of four religions—Hinduism, Jainism, Buddhism, and

Sikhism whose devotees together constitute about 25 percent devotees of the world's population. India has about 300,000 mosques, which is more than the number of mosques in all the Islamic countries. Martial arts and yoga are other the gifts India has given to the world.

In India, as in most Asian countries, culture is defined by ethnicity, traditions, festivals, language, and dance. This is in contrast to the Western definition of culture, which is defined to a large extent by honesty, discipline, cleanliness, etiquette, and principles of equal justice.

Some deep-rooted generalizations about India:

- India is predominantly a land of elephants, snakes, and cows
- India is all about holy men, rites, and rituals
- India is backward and underdeveloped
- India is *Bollywood*: the Indian film industry
- India is dirty, unorganized, and corrupt
- India is steeped in poverty
- Women are not at all empowered in India
- Women are unsafe in India

India is in fact a land of contrasting cultures. On the one hand, there is the urban, educated, English-speaking, well-to-do Indian; on the other is the rural, unemployed, uneducated, local dialect-speaking Indian who does not even have access to the basic necessities of life. Then, there is the metro city Indian and the small-city Indian. The average metro city Indian is urbane, sophisticated, well heeled, and widely traveled. The small-town Indian is now aspiring to attain those comforts. Paradoxically, values of both groups collide. While the latter boasts of strong middle-class values (deeply religious, abstaining from premarital sex, dating, drinking, or other such vices), the former is experimental and enjoys the so-called pleasures of life. Live-in relationships, dating, and illicit liaisons are frowned upon in Indian society, and those indulging in the same are accused of succumbing to the westernization of Indian culture.

Things also change across states. In the states of north India, it is advisable for females to dress more conservatively unlike in the state of Gujarat in western India, where it is not a big deal to wear jeans, tight-fitting clothes, skirts, and shorts. Public display of affection is still not common in small towns, but widely catching on in big metro cities.

India is steeped in ritualism, and some change is occurring in that respect. For instance, after marriage, a Hindu wife has to observe several *fasts* (abstaining from eating food) for the safety and protection of her sons and husband. Most empowered females now do not observe so many fasts. Girls and boys in India traditionally have been segregated, and arranged marriages are still usually the norm. The birth of a boy is celebrated, while the birth of a girl, in many households, is still a cause of sorrow and resentment. Interreligion and intercaste marriages are exceptions rather than the norms. In some small towns and villages, the bride and the bridegroom do not even see each other before marriage. The custom of child marriages is still prevalent in some parts of rural India. Things are changing for the better for Indian women, as illustrated by the picture alongside, which depicts the inauguration of the Bharatiya Mahila Bank, India's first state-owned women's bank, in Mumbai, Maharashtra (*The New York Times,* 2013).

Rituals and traditions are considered quite important in India. All the major events in the various stages of life (such as the birth of a child, puberty in males, marriage, etc.) are celebrated with a ritual, and therefore priests are placed on a high pedestal as they are the ones authorized to perform the *puja* (prayer) or the *havan* (lighting of the ceremonial fire along with chanting of sacred hymns). Dying on a hospital bed is not

A bank for women by women

considered good; so, dying persons are usually placed on the floor. It is believed that putting a few drops of sacred water from the river Ganges in the dying person's mouth will lead to reincarnation of the soul after death.

Even though India has a rich historical past, most Indians are strong believers in mythology. Indeed many of their festivals are intertwined with myths. It is quite common for representatives of religious groups to file petitions in court to ban books, cinema, and songs that they feel in some way or the other violate their religious and cultural beliefs. Differences also exist in the practice of different religious faiths and customs. Some tribes and local communities in India practice customs that would be considered prehistoric by even the standards of the average educated Indian. There is a religious tribunal called *khap panchayat* in the state of Haryana in north India that dictates how village girls should dress, whom they should marry, and whether they can even carry a cell phone. The *Agora* tribe in Benares eats the remains of dead people that float on the Ganges River.

Recently, a petition was issued by the Bombay High Court to Indian filmmaker Sanjay Leela Bhansali to change the title of the film *Ram Leela* as it "hurts Hindu sentiments." The petitioner is Sandeep Shukla who is the vice president of the Shree Maharashtra Ramleela Mandal, which organizes the *Ramleela* performance—based on the epic, *Ramayana*. Every year in October, Indians celebrate the nine-day fasting period of *Navratri*, which celebrates the defeat of Raavan, the demon king, at the hands of Lord Ram, the mythical king of Ayodhya. The petition states that the film posters of the film offended Hindu sentiments as they contained "vulgar, rude, offensive dialogue" and "objectionable scenes which degrade the religious feelings." The court refused to block the release of the film, which was released on the November 17, 2013 (the film is running successfully in India currently).

Source: IndiaToday.in (November 13, 2013).

Customs differ across states of India, and the northern states of Punjab, Haryana, New Delhi, and Uttar Pradesh are more patriarchal. The southern states (Tamil Nadu, Karnataka, Kerala, and Andhra Pradesh) in contrast, are more broadminded than the states of north India. Eastern India (West Bengal, Orissa, Tripura, etc.) is less patriarchal, while western

India (Maharashtra, Gujarat, Goa) is more liberal and cosmopolitan than the rest of India.

Consumption spending is rising in India, though the findings are skewed toward the urban rich. Recent data on consumption pattern by the National Sample Survey Organisation (NSSO) shows that the richest 10 percent of the Indian society have recorded the highest growth (around 50 to 60 percent) while the poorest 10 percent have seen the slowest growth (around 20 to 30 percent) in incomes. The rest of the 80 percent people have seen roughly the same levels of growth (around 30 to 40 percent). In 2012, a rural poor person was spending just Indian rupee (INR) 521 per month in comparison to the rural rich person who spent INR 4,481 per month. The urban poor person spent INR 700 per month, while the urban rich person spent close to INR 11,000 per month. The SAARC India Country Report reveals that poverty in India has declined from 45 percent in 1993 through 1994 to 21.9 percent in 2011 through 2012. Teledensity has increased considerably in India. In March 2012, it was 78.66 percent as compared to 70.89 percent in March 2011. The wireless subscriber base in India was 919.17 million in March 2012 and the Internet subscriber base stood at 22.86 million, registering an annual growth rate of about 16.19 percent. The worker participation rate for women was 21.9 percent in 2011 and 2012, and the mean age for marriage of women stood at 19.5 years.

Work Culture in India

The Indian work culture and communication styles vary across the various sectors. The traditional manufacturing firms are very different from the newer sectors such as hospitality, IT-enabled services, telecom, and banking. While the former is more hierarchical and formal, the latter is more flexible and technologically advanced. The generic aspects common to most Indian organizations are enumerated as follows.

Strongly Hierarchical

In the Indian society, age and position are held in high reverence. People do not disagree forcefully with the boss. A senior is addressed as sir or ma'am and not by name. Career advancement is by seniority rather than by accomplishment and the superior plays a major role in this.

Greg Chappell, former coach of the Indian cricket team, blamed the Indian culture for their poor performance in cricket. Indian culture is not a team culture, he is reported to have said. In the Indian culture, it is wiser to keep your head down so that nobody can "knock it off." According to him, the Indian side lacked leaders because they could not take responsibility for their decisions. He blamed this on the parents, coaches, and schoolteachers who made all the decisions themselves.

Source: The Economics Times (March 7, 2012).

Relationship Driven

Organizational relationships are the highest priority. Tasks and goals are important to the extent that relationships are not jeopardized. There might be a distinction between surface communication and true intention. Decision making is joint and usually by consensus. The senior person must be involved in the decision-making process. Interaction is formal and follows a ritualized process. There is a strong reliance on face-to-face communication. Growth in the organization is judged on the basis of relationships rather than on merit or performance. The work culture is slightly informal, with workers' personal and professional lives intertwined with each other.

People Oriented

People form the mainstay of the Indian organizational culture. Processes are important, but subordinate to relationships with people. Rules, regulations, and job descriptions are not very explicit. Unlike in the West, Indians place a high premium on the number of man-hours put into the work per day. Working overtime for free is expected and encouraged. Employees thus are not free to go home when their work is over.

Deadlines

Indians are not very punctual. It is normal for everyone to trickle in long after the meeting has started. Project schedules and timelines may also be extended. It is important, therefore, to emphasize the value of deadlines and ask for feedback intermittently. Business processes are also slow in India. Decision making is unhurried and one has to visit a number of times to finalize a deal. A no should not be interpreted as a final no. Persuasiveness can convert the no to a yes.

Office Leave and Vacation

Indians work long hours, and the concept of a weekend break does not exist in India. Indians value their festival time and may take leave during the two to three major festivals of India such as Dussehra, Diwali (October–November), and Id (twice a year). Indians, especially those that migrate to big cities for work, may like also to have frequent breaks from work on public holidays including Independence Day, Gandhi Jayanti, Rakshabandhan, and Bhai-dooj.

Social Invitations

In India, one may be invited to a colleague's house for social functions such as a housewarming party, a Diwali party, marriage celebrations, and anniversary parties; it is customary to attend. Flowers may be gifted, or a small token may be given to the host. It is a good idea to praise the arrangements made by the host.

Giving and Receiving Feedback

Indians are indirect communicators and do not like to offend the other person. Feedback is given in a rather roundabout manner, and it is up to the listener to comprehend what the speaker really wants to say. Of course, in the private sector, things are slightly different but this is generally the case. When giving feedback it would be wiser to say words to the effect of "You have tremendous scope for improvement" instead of saying outright that the work is not up to the mark.

Body Language

The handshake is a common form of greeting between men. Indians also believe in formal exchange of business cards. Sometimes a close hug is also acceptable if the parties know each other. Women in general do not shake hands with men unless they are also westernized in their thinking and approach. It is wise to do a *namaste*, which is a traditional form of greeting when meeting Indian professional women. Dressing is formal for both men and women. Indians also value personal space (generally an arm's length). It is common to see Indian men and women of the same gender hold hands in a casual manner. A smile, a head nod (up and down or side to side), and a figure "8" movement of the head indicate consent and agreement. The right hand is considered cleaner than the left hand and should be used to pass around things to other people. Putting feet up, touching the head, and pointing are considered inappropriate gestures.

Business Etiquette

Business can be discussed over corporate lunches and dinners, which usually take place in well-known hotels or restaurants. Spouses usually attend social and business gatherings in the night. Orthodox Hindus, Muslims, and women do not consume alcohol during official functions. It is customary to arrive late to a function. It is not an obligation to empty the plate. One must be prepared for intrusive questions.

Many Indians working abroad are quite adaptive and responsive to the cultures of the other nations. In fact, many appreciate the working style practiced in these countries.

"Internationally, the emphasis is more on the quality of work" says Darshan Shroff, Director, PPJ Shroff Securities Pvt. Ltd., who has also worked with JPMorgan Chase & Co., London, and Barclays Capital, New York. Says designer Pria Kataria Puri who is now based in Kuwait,

"The work culture internationally is far more productive and cost effective than India. There are various reasons why working here is productive. Every indoor space is centrally air conditioned, whether it is the office, car, bus, malls, or shops. So the working environment is pleasant... The three hour rest period (between 1 p.m. and 4 p.m.) helps a person work more efficiently."

Source: Sharma (2013).

Visitors to India can benefit from the following information:

- Do not enter an Indian house with shoes on, especially in western India. Always ask for the host's preference.
- It is better to know the food preferences of Indians in advance as onions and garlic are not used by many.
- Refrain from consuming meat and alcohol in the open and during the day.
- Do not eat with the same hand used for serving food; also do not eat and drink from somebody else's plate or glass.
- Do not eat food from roadside stalls and always carry bottled water.
- Do not violate the rules of sacred temples.
- Treat books as sacred; so do not walk over them or throw them on the floor.
- Avoid discussing religion, especially with Muslims.
- Avoid interacting with saints and *sadhus*, unless verified by somebody else.
- Expect to bargain with street vendors and hawkers, as they customarily charge at least 50 percent extra for foreigners.
- Do not thumb rides from unknown people and always stay in well-known and certified hotels.
- Dress modestly, covering the arms, torso, and legs.
- Exercise care on Indian roads.
- Make sure you have a travel and health insurance when traveling to India.

- Ensure immunizations are up to date before arriving in India, including those against diseases like typhoid, malaria, hepatitis, and tetanus.
- Smile freely; people are always willing to help and guide a foreigner. Adaptable and adjusting, they are also forgiving when foreigners make mistakes.

E.M. Forster rightly described India in his book *A Passage to India* as both a muddle and a mystery. There is a certain mystique to India. It has a wondrous quality because of its richness in terms of diversity, duality, and diaspora. One can never be sure of what's in store. India defies labeling. A panoramic delight, nature and mankind seamlessly integrate in India to provide a sensory treat to the visitor. Truly incredible!

In conclusion, it would not be incorrect to say that India is still evolving. It is a country in a state of cultural and social transition. There is a definite paradigm shift from the narrow parochialism that existed during my grandfather's time to the moderate thinking practiced by my parents and my own liberal attitude. There is a sea change in perspective especially brought about by Internet penetration, globalization, and greater media accessibility. But that is the urban side of the story; a sizeable population, about 72 percent of the rural hinterland is still defined by family, caste, or community, gender, religion, region, and language. This, people say, is the real India.

In the course of writing this book, I realized that most of the Western countries that I researched (and visited) had well-developed systems to safeguard individual rights and privileges. India has a long way to go to develop such systems, given our cultural mindset that still permeates the social fabric of our lives. Change is a slow process, and cultural change is the most difficult to bring about. Until then, India would continue to be labeled as a paradox, a wonder, and a bundle of contradictions.

References

AFP. *Bill Gates 'disrespects' South Korean President with Casual Handshake*, April 23, 2013, http://www.telegraph.co.uk/technology/bill-gates/10011847/Bill-Gates-disrespects-South-Korean- president-with-casual-handshake.html (accessed October 7, 2013).

Akre, B.S. *Daimler-Chrysler Merger Provides Lessons in German Culture.* Associated Press, October 17, 1998, http://old.chronicle.augusta.com/stories/1998/10/17/bus_242108.shtml

Associated Press. *Mahmoud Ahmadinejad under fire for hugging Hugr Chavez's mother*, 2013, http://nbclatino.com/2013/03/12/ahmadinejad-under-fire-for-hugging-hugo-chavezs-mother/, (accessed March 13, 2013).

ASTD. *Global Relocation Trends for 2012*, August 08, 2012, http://www.astd.org/Publications/Blogs/Global-HRD-Blog/2012/08/Global-Relocation-Trends-for-2012

The Canadian Press. *Baird Allegedly Made 'Inappropriate and Derogatory Remarks' to Maldives Official*, October 7, 2013, http://www2.macleans.ca/2013/10/07/baird-allegedly-made-inappropriate-and-derogatory-remarks-to-Maldives-official/

c JETRO. *Communicating with Japanese in Business*, 1999, http://www.jetro.go.jp/costarica/mercadeo/communicationwith.pdf

Carol, L. "A Mad Tea Party." In *Alice's Adventures in Wonderland*. London, UK: Macmillan, 1865.

Census India, 2010–2011, http://censusindia.gov.in/

Chang, L.-C. "The Negotiation Styles of Overseas Chinese: A Comparison of Taiwanese and Indonesian Chinese Patterns." *African Journal of Business Management* 5, no. 20 (September 2011), pp. 8079–87.

Charles, M. "Language Matters In Global Communication." *Journal of Business Communication* 44, no. 3 (July 2007), pp. 260–82.

Chentsova-Dutton, Y.E.; and A. Vaughn. "Let Me Tell You What to Do: Cultural Differences in Advice-Giving." *Journal of Cross-Cultural Psychology* 20, no. 10 (June 2011), pp. 1–17.

Chua-Eoan, H. "The Queen and Mrs. Obama: A Breach in Protocol." *Time magazine*, April 1, 2009, http://www.time.com/time/world/article/0,8599,1888962,00.html#ixzz2TLgr19v2

Crystal, D. *English as a Global Language*. Cambridge, MA: Cambridge University Press, 1997.

De Mente, B.L. *Korean Etiquette and Ethics in Business*. Lincolnwood, IL: NTC Business Books, 1994.

Earley, C.; and S. Ang (2003). *Cultural Intelligence: Individual Interactions Across Cultures*. Stanford, CA: Stanford University Press, 2003.

Economist Intelligence Unit. *Competing Across Borders: How Cultural and Communication Barriers Affect,* April 25, 2012, EF Education First: http://www.economistinsights.com/countries-trade-investment/analysis/competing-across-borders (accessed October 18, 2013).

The Economics Times. *Greg Chappell Attacks Indian Culture And Cricket Team*, March 7, 2012, articles.economictimes.indiatimes.com/2012-03-07/news/31132209_1_indian-culture-cricket-team-greg-chappell

Feilin, L.; and Gaofeng, Y. "Cultural Differences in Compliments." *Canadian Social Science* 1, no. 1 (May 2005), pp. 68–72.

France protects itself. *"Mail Online.* Associated Newspapers Ltd, n.d. Web. 1 Mar. 2013. http://www.dailymail.co.uk/news/article-530403/France-protects-dreaded-English-language-banning-fast-food-podcasting.html

George, O.; and O. Owoyemi. "Impact of National Culture on the Management of Multinational Businesses: The Case of Cadbury Worldwide." *International Journal of Business and Management Tomorrow* 2, no. 7 (July 2012), www.ijbmt.com

Goodall, K.; N. Li; and M. Warner. *Expatriate Managers in China: The Influence of Chinese Culture on Cross-Cultural Management*. Judge Business School, University of Cambridge, Working Paper Series, January 2007.

Graddol, D. *The Future of English*. London, UK: The British Council, 1997.

Grecke, A.G.; and G. House. "The Relationship Between National Culture and TMT Demographic Heterogeneity." *Singapore Management Review* 34, no. 2 (July 2012), pp. 58–69.

Hall, E. T. *The Hidden Dimension*. Garden City, NY: Doubleday, 1966.

Hall, E.T. "The Silent Language in Overseas Business." *Harvard Business Review* 38, no. 3 (May 1960), pp. 87–96.

Hall, E.T. *The Silent Language*. Garden City, NY: Doubleday, 1959.

Henderson, D. *Inside the Japanese Matrix,* June 2012, http://deanhenderson.wordpress.com/2012/06/03/inside-the-japanese-matrix/; http://theintelhub.com/2012/11/30/underestimating-japans-nuclear-disaster/

Hills, M.D. "Kluckhohn and Strodtbeck's Values Orientation Theory." *Online Readings in Psychology and Culture* 4, no. 4 (August 2002), http://dx.doi.org/10.9707/2307-0919.1040

Hofstede, G. "The Cultural Relativity of Organizational Practices and Theories." *Journal of International Business Studies* 14, no. 2 (Autumn 1983), pp. 75–89. Special Issue on Cross-Cultural Management http://www.jstor.org/stable/222593

Hofstede, G. *Culture's Consequences: International Differences in Work-Related Values*. Beverly Hills, CA: Sage, 1980.

Hofstede, G. *Cultures and Organizations Software of the Mind. Intercultural Cooperation and its Importance for Survival.* New York, NY: McGraw-Hill, 1997.

Hofstede, G. *Cultures and Organizations: Software of the Mind.* London, UK: McGraw-Hill, 1991.

Hofstede, G.; and G.J. Hofstede. *Cultures and Organizations—Software of the Mind.* 2nd ed. New York, NY: McGraw-Hill, 2005.

Hofstede, G.; Hofstede, G.J.; and Minkov, M. *Cultures and Organizations: Software of the Mind.* 3rd ed. New York, NY: McGrawHill, 2010.

Hoft, N.L. "Developing a Communication Model." In *International User Interface*, eds. E.M. del Galdo; and J. Nielson. New York, NY: Wiley Computer Publishing.

IndiaToday.in. *Bombay High Court refuses to stay release of Ram Leela*, November 13, 2013, http://indiatoday.intoday.in/story/bombay-high-court-refuses-to-stay-release-of-ram-leela/1/324643.html

Johnson, F. "Agreement and Disagreement: A Cross-Cultural Comparison." *BISAL* 1 (2006), pp. 41–67, http://www.bisal.bbk.ac.uk/publications/volume1/pdf/Fiona_Johnson_pdf

Journal of Extension. *Welcome to the Journal of Extension,* n.d., www.joe.org/

Kluckhohn, F.R.; and F.L. Strodtbeck. *Variations in Value Orientations.* Westport, CT: Greenwood Press, 1961.

Kobayashi, J.; and L. Viswat. "Intercultural Communication Competence in Business: Communication Between Japanese and Americans." *Journal of Intercultural Communication* no. 26 (July 2011), p. 1.

Lahiri, T. "How Tech, Individuality Shape Hinglish." *The Wall Street Journal*, January 21, 2012.

Lassiter, J.E. "African Culture and Personality: Bad Social Science, Effective Social Activism, or a Call to Reinvent Ethnology?" *African Studies Quarterly* 3, no. 2 (1999), p. 1, http://asq.africa.ufl.edu/v3/v3i3a1.htm

LeBaron, M. *Culture-Based Negotiation Styles. Beyond Intractability*, July 2003, http://www.beyondintractability.org, (accessed August 23, 2013).

Lundquist, L. *Humour as a Mediator in Cross-Cultural Professional Settings. Examples from Danish and French.* Working paper no. 66. International Center for Business and Politics Copenhagen Business School, 2009.

Meghan Peterson Fenn. *Is giving parenting advice in Britain taboo*, 2012, http://www.bringingupbrits.co.uk/blog/is-giving-parenting-advice-in-britain-taboo

Mainela, T.; and T. Mustonen. *Workshop paper submitted to the 34th EIBA Annual Conference*, Tallinn, Estonia, December 11–13, 2008.

Mann, L.; M. Radford; P. Burnett; S. Ford; M. Bond; K. Leung; H. Nakamura; G. Vaughan; and K. Yang. "Cross-Cultural Differences in Self-Reported Decision-Making Style and Confidence." *International Journal of Psychology* 33, no. 5 (October 1998), pp. 325–35.

Meritt, A. *News Report in the Telegraph.* (March 20, 2013).

Nakane, I. *Silence in the Multicultural Classroom: Perceptions and Performance.* Amsterdam: John Benjamins, 2007.

The New York Times. *Image of the Day*, November 19, 2013, India.blogs.nytimes .com/2013/11/19/image-of-the-day-november-19/?_r=0

Nishiyama, K. "Barriers to International Business Communication." In *Doing Business with Japan: Successful Strategies for Intercultural Communication.* Honolulu, HI: University of Hawaii press, 2000.

Norman, L. *How to Express Agreement and Disagreement in English*, n.d., http:// www.ehow.com/how_6785120_express-agreement-disagreement-english .html#ixzz2NyWf9YlB

Reynolds, S.; and D. Valentine. *Guide to Cross-Cultural Communications.* In ed. M.Munter, 2nd ed. Upper Saddle River, NJ: Prentice Hall, 2011.

Samovar, L.A.; and R.E. Porter. *Communication Between Cultures.* 4th ed., Belmont, CA: Wadsworth, 2001.

Schwartz, S.H. "A Theory of Cultural Values and Some Implications for Work." *Applied Psychology: An International Review* 48, no. 1 (January 1999), pp. 23–47. doi:10.1111/j.1464-0597.1999.tb00047.x

Schwartz, S.H. "Are There Universal Aspects in the Structure and Contents of Human Values?" *Journal of Social Issues* 50, no. 4 (Winter 1994), pp. 19–45. doi:10.1111/j.1540-4560.1994.tb01196.x

Sharma, G. P. *Understanding the World Business Culture*, October 7, 2013, http:// timesofindia.indiatimes.com/life-style/relationships/work/Understanding-the-world-business-culture/articleshow/17191117.cms

Simon, S. *France pushes common English term out of French lexicon*, 2013, http:// www.npr.org/2013/01/26/170336339/france-pushes-common-english-term-out-of-french-lexicon, (accessed January 31, 2013).

Spencer-Oatey, H. *Culturally Speaking: Managing Rapport Through Talk Across Cultures.* 2000. New York, NY: Cassel Academic

Tannen, D. "The Pragmatics of Cross-Cultural Communication." *Applied Linguistics* 5, no. 3 (1984), pp. 189–95, http://xa.yimg.com/kq/ groups/23344266/839912215/name/the_pragmatics_of_cross-cultural_ communication.pdf

Tarpley, W.G.; and A. Chaitkin. *George Bush: The Unauthorized Biography*, 651. San Diego, CA: Progressive Press paperback edition, 2004. Web link to Chapter -XXV- Thyroid Storm, January 3, 1992.

The Telegraph. *Barack Obama Criticised for 'treasonous' Bow to Japanese Emperor*, November 16, 2009, http://www.telegraph.co.uk/news/worldnews/ barackobama/6580190/Barack-Obama-criticised-for-treasonous-bow-to-Japanese-emperor.html

Thomas, M.P. April 15, 2013. "Putting the Shine Back Into Tata Steel." *India Forbes*, http://india.forbes.com/article/boardroom/putting-the-shine back-into-tata-steel/35049/0#ixzz2zXeQHbW3 (April 19, 2013)

Trompenaars, F. Riding the Waves of Culture: Understanding Cultural Diversity in Business. London, UK: Economist Books, 1993.

Trudeau, P. "Trudeau's Pirouette." *Iconic Photos*, May 7, 1977, http://iconicphotos.wordpress.com/2009/06/19/trudeaus-pirouette/

Unnithan, C. "U.S. Food Giants Turn Vegetarian in Gujarat." The Times of India, March 6, 2013.

Warren, J. "The Politics of Good Touch, Bad Touch." *The New York Times*, July 23, 2006, http://www.nytimes.com/2006/07/23/fashion/sundaystyles/23touch.html?_r=0; http://www.worldalmanac.com/blog/2007/01/22/bush-merkel.jpg

Wolfson, N. "An empirically Based Analysis of Complimenting in American English." In *Sociolinguistics and Language Acquisition*, eds. N. Wolfson; and E. Judd, 82–95. Rowley: Newbury House, 1983.

Woo, H.S.; and C. Prud'homme. "Cultural Characteristics Prevalent in the Chinese Negotiation Process." *European Business Review* 99, no. 5 (1999), 313–22

Zipperer, J. "Global Languages Aren't Universal." *Internet World* 7, no. 12 (June 2001), pp. 14–5.

Suggestions for Further Reading

Websites

- http://www.intercultural.org/books.php#general
- http://ccat.sas.upenn.edu/~haroldfs/bibliogs/CROSCULT.HTM
- http://www.intercultural.org/books.php#teams
- Richard Lewis: http://www.crossculture.com/home/
- http://blog.crossculture.com/
- http://www.soberit.hut.fi/gecos/deliverables/Cross-Cultural-Teams.pdf
- http://www.cgdev.org/doc/2013_MiddleClassIndia_Technical-Note_CGDNote.pdf
- The World Bank. *PovcalNet: An Online Poverty Analysis Tool*, 2013, http://iresearch.worldbank.org/PovcalNet, (accessed October 27, 2013)
- http://www.ncaer.org/downloads/MediaClips/Press/yahoo-rich-households-o.pdf
- Salacuse, J. *Top Ten Ways That Culture Can Affect Your Negotiation*, 2004, Ivey Business Journal: http://iveybusinessjournal.com/topics/the-organization/negotiating-the- top-ten-ways-that-culture-can-affect-your-negotiation#.UiWtKhtpnv4
- Sebenius, J.A. "Assess, Don't Assume, Part I. Etiquette and National Culture in Negotiation." (Working paper 10-048), *Harvard Business School, 2009,* http://www.hbs.edu/faculty/Publication%20Files/10-048.pdf
- Shekhar, E & Sharma, V. 2011. Cross border mergers in light of the fallout of the Bharti-MTN deal. NUJS L Review, 99 http://nujslawreview.org/pdf/articles/2011_1/esha-shekhar.pdf

- The New York Times. *Etiquette & Behavior,* 2009, http://www.nytimes.com/fodors/top/features/travel/destinations/asia/japan/tokyo/fdrs_feat_156_5.html?n=Top%2FFeatures%2FTravel%2FDestinations%2FAsia%2FJapan%2FTokyo, (accessed October 10, 2013).
- Kuntz, T. *Word for Word/Drinking Etiquette Abroad; How to Succeed in Business By Getting Really Bombed,* October 26, 1997, The New York Times: http://www.nytimes.com/1997/10/26/weekinreview/word-for-word-drinking-etiquette-abroad-succeed-business-getting-really-bombed.html?pagewanted=all&src=pm, (accessed October 10, 2013).
- Mohn, T. *Going Global, Stateside,* March 08, 2010, The New York Times: http://www.nytimes.com/2010/03/09/business/global/09training.html, (accessed October 10, 2013).
- S. Varma. "Income Disparity Between Rich and Poor Growing Rapidly." *NSSO Report on Consumption Spending,* July 28, 2013, http://articles.timesofindia.indiatimes.com/2013-07-28/india/40848406_1_urban-areas-rural-areas-disparity, (accessed on January 01, 2014).
- SAARC. "SAARC Development Goals." *India Country Report 2013: Statistical Appraisal,* 2013, http://mospi.nic.in/mospi_new/upload/SAARC_Development_Goals_%20India_Country_Report_29aug13.pdf, (accessed on January 01, 2014).
- Lorenz, E. and N. Lazaric. "The Transferability of Business Practices and Problem-Solving Skills to Japanese Firms in Britain and France". Financed by the DG12 of the European Commission Under its Targeted *Socio-Economic Research (TSER) Programme,* (Contract No. SOEI – CT97-1078), 2000, http://www.druid.dk/uploads/tx_picturedb/ds2000-112.pdf
- Linköping Institute of Technology. *Decision Making in On-Site Operations Coordination Centers Final Report,* Division of Industrial Ergonomics, Linköping Institute of Technology, https://www.msb.se/Upload/Kunskapsbank/Forskningsrapporter/Slutrapporter/2009%20Bridging%20Cultural%20Barrier s%20to%20Collaborative%20Decision.pdf

- http://www.amazon.com/gp/richpub/syltguides/fullview/ RECU02EJ6QWMC

Websites with Videos

- **Guest Videos**: http://www.kwintessential.co.uk/intercultural/ diversity-videos.html
- *The Intercultural Film Database*: http://www.uni-hildesheim.de/ interculturalfilm/
- *Institute of Intercultural Communication*, University of Hildesheim, Marienburger Platz 22, 31141 Hildesheim, Germany
- http://teachpsych.org/resources/Documents/otrp/resources/hil-l98activities.pdf
- Roell, C. *Intercultural Training with Films*, 2010, http://files.eric .ed.gov/fulltext/EJ914887.pdf
- http://www.iaccp.org/teaching/films/bennett.pdf

Research Articles of Interest

- Graham, J.L. "Brazilian, Japanese, and American Business Negotiations." *Journal of International Business Studies*, 14, no. 1 (March 1983), pp. 47–61.
- Tannen, D. "The Pragmatics of Cross-Cultural Communication." *Applied Linguistics*, 5, no. 3 (1984b), pp. 189–195.
- Hofstede, G. "Cultural Differences in Teaching and Learning." *International Journal of Intercultural Relations* 10, no. 3 (1986), pp. 301–320.
- Kopper, E. "Swiss and Germans: Similarities and Differences in Work-Related Values, Attitudes, and Behavior." *International Journal of Intercultural Relations* 17, no. 2 (Spring 1993), pp. 167–184.
- Reynolds, B.K. "A Cross-Cultural Study of Values of Germans and Americans." *International Journal of Intercultural Relations* 8, no. 3 (1984), pp. 269–278.

- Adelman, M.P.; and M.W. Lustig. "Intercultural Communication Problems as Perceived by Saudi Arabian and American Managers." *International Journal of Intercultural Relations* 5, no. 4 (1981), pp. 349–363.
- Aune, R.K.; and L.L. Waters. "Cultural Differences in Deception: Motivations to Deceive in Samoans and North Americans." *International Journal of Intercultural Relations* 18, no. 2 (Spring 1994), pp. 159–172.
- Barnlund, D.C.; and S. Araki. "Intercultural Encounters: The Management of Compliments by Japanese and Americans." *Journal of Cross-Cultural Psychology* 16, no. 1 (March 1985), pp. 9–26.
- Barnlund, D.C.; and M. Yoshioka. "Apologies: Japanese and American Styles." *International Journal of Intercultural Relations* 14, no. 2 (1990), pp. 193–206.
- Cohen, R. "Problems of Intercultural Communication in Egyptian-American Diplomatic Relations." *International Journal of Intercultural Relations* 11, no. 1 (1987), pp. 29–47.
- Sanchez, J.; and M.E. Stuckey. "Communicating Culture Through Leadership: One View From Indian Country." *Communication Studies* 50, no. 2 (Summer 1999), pp. 103–115.
- Bumpus, M.A. "Using Motion Pictures to Teach Management: Refocusing the Camera Lens Through the Infusion Approach to Diversity." *Journal of Management Education* 29, no. 6 (December 2005), pp. 792–815.
- *Article*, http://www.brown.uk.com/teaching/intercultural/briam.pdf
- Vanishree V.M.; MAPL; and M.A. ELT. "Provision for Linguistic Diversity and Linguistic Minorities in India – Masters Dissertation." *Language in India* 11, no. 2 (February 2011), http://www.languageinindia.com/feb2011/vanishreemastersfinal.pdf, (accessed January 31, 2013).
- Güss, C.D. "Fire and Ice: Testing a Model on Culture and Complex Problem Solving." *Journal of Cross-Cultural Psychology* 42, no. 7 (October 2011), pp. 1279–1298, http://jcc.sagepub.com/content/42/7/1279.full.pdf

- Limaye, M. R.; and D.A. Victor. "Cross-Cultural Business Communication Research: State of the Art and Hypotheses for the 1990s." *Journal of Business Communication* 28, no. 3 (June 1991), pp. 277–299.
- Cardon P.W. "A Critique of Hall's Contexting Model: A Meta-Analysis of Literature." *Journal of Business and Technical Communication* 22, no. 4 (October 2008), pp. 399–428, http://jbt.sagepub.com/content/22/4/399
- Tompkins D.; D. Galbraith; and P. Tompkins. "Universalism, Particularism and Cultural Self-Awareness: a Comparison of American and Turkish university students." *Journal of International Business and Cultural Studies* 3, pp. 1–8, http://www.aabri.com/manuscripts/09324.pdf
- Triandis, C.H.; R. Bontempo; J.M. Villareal; M. Asai; and N. Lucca. "Individualism and Collectivism: Cross-Cultural Perspectives on Self-Ingroup Relationships." *Journal of Personality and Social Psychology* 54, no. 2 (February 1988), pp. 323–338, http://www.radford.edu/~jaspelme/_private/gradsoc_articles/individualism_collectivism/individualism_collectivism_1988.pdf
- Aldridge, J.M.; B.J. Fraser; P.C. Taylor; and C. Chen. "Constructivist Learning Environments in a Cross-National Study in Taiwan and Australia." *International Journal of Science Education* 22, no. 1 (2000), pp. 37–55.
- *Forbes.* 174, no. 11 (2004), p. 39, 1c.
- Hobson, E.; and Bohonh. "The Effects of Culture on Student Questioning in the Science Classroom." *Journal of Cross – Disciplinary Perspectives in Education* 4, no. 1 (May 2011), pp. 41–50, Bohonhttp://jcpe.wmwikis.net/file/view/hobsonbohon.pdf
- Lee, M-H.; C-Y. Chang; and C-C. Tsai. "Exploring Taiwanese High School Students' Perceptions of and Preferences for Teacher Authority in the Earth Science Classroom With Relation to Their Attitudes and Achievement." *International Journal of Science Education* 31, no. 13 (September 2009), pp. 1811–1830.

- Reimann, A. "Intercultural Communication and the Essence of Humour." *Journal of the Faculty of International Studies* 29, (2010), pp. 23–34
- Thomas, J. "Cross-Cultural Pragmatic Failure." *Applied Linguistics* 4, no. 2 (1983) 91–112.
- Wolfson, N. "Compliments in Cross-Cultural Perspective." *TESOL Quarterly* 15, no. 2 (1981), pp. 117–124.
- Wolfson, N. "An Empirically Based Analysis of Complimenting in American English." In *Sociolinguistics and Language Learning,* eds. N. Wolfson; and E. Judd (pp. 82–95). Rowley, MA: Newbury House Publishing, Inc.
- Wolfson, N. *Canadian Social Science* 1, no. 1 (May 2005).
- Sree, P.S.; and Siawuk, Y.A. "Awareness of Proxemics for effective Inter- Cultural Communication: The Case of Gamo People of Ethiopia." *Research Expo International. Multidisciplinary Research Journal* 2, no. 3 (September 2012), pp. 16–23, www.researchjournals.in
- Pratt-Johnson, Y. "Communicating Cross-Culturally: What Teachers Should Know." *The Internet TESL Journal*, http://iteslj.org/Articles/Pratt-Johnson-CrossCultural.html
- Gupta, A.K.; and V. Govindarajan. "Knowledge Flows Within Multinational Corporations." *Strategic Management Journal* 21, no. 4 (April 2000), pp. 473–496.
- Selmer, J. "Language Ability and Adjustment: Western Expatriates in China", *Thunderbird International Business Review* 48, no. 3 (May–June 2006), pp. 347–368, Wiley InterScience, www.interscience.wiley.com
- Ko, H.; and M. Yang. "The Effects of Cross-Cultural Training on Expatriate Assignments." *Intercultural Communication Studies* 20, no. 1 (June 2011), pp. 158–174.
- Sriussadaporn, R. "Managing International Business Communication Problems at Work: A Pilot Study in Foreign Companies in Thailand." *Cross Cultural Management: An International Journal* 13, no. 4 (October 2006), pp. 330–344.

- Appelbaum, H.S.; J. Roberts; and T.B. Shapiro. "Cultural Strategies in M&As: Investigating Ten Case Studies." *Journal of Executive Education 8*, no. (1) (2009). pp. 33–58.
- Burt, R.S. "The Culture Effect." *Chicago GSB 2*, no.1 (2000). Cisco IT Case Study Acquisition Integration www.cisco.com/go/ciscoit
- Hollmann, J.; A. Carpes; and T.A. Beuron (2010) the Daimler Chrysler merger- a cultural mismatch? 3 Rev. Adm. UFSM, Santa Maria, v. 3, n. 3, p. 431- 440, set./dez. 2010. Recebidoem 03.09.10 / Aceitoem 08.12.10
- Boulgarides, J.; and D. Oh. "A comparison of Japanese, Korean and American Managerial Decision Styles: An Exploratory Study." *Leadership and Organizational Development Journal 6*, no. 1 (1985), pp. 9–11.
- Chu, P.C.; E.E. Spires; and T. Sueyoshi. "Cross-Cultural Differences in Choice Behavior and Use of Decision Aids: a Comparison of Japan and the United States." *Organizational Behavior and Human Decision Processes 77*, no. 2 (February 1999), pp. 147–170.
- Hofstede, G. "Asian Management in the 21st Century." *Asia Pacific Journal of Management 24*, no. 4 (December 2007), pp. 411–420.
- Schramm-Nielsen, J. "Cultural Dimensions of Decision Making: Denmark and France Compared." *Journal of Managerial Psychology 16*, no. 6 (August 2001), pp. 404–423.
- Kiss, G. "Managing Cross-Cultural Communication Challenges Toward a More Perfect Union in an Age of Diversity." *Aarms Communications 4*, no. 2 (2005), pp. 215–223, http://www.zmne.hu/aarms/docs/Volume4/Issue2/pdf/02kiss.pdf
- Adachi, Y. "Business Negotiations Between the Americans and the Japanese," *Global Business Languages 2*, no. 4 (1997), http://docs.lib.purdue.edu/gbl/vol2/iss1/4
- Brett, J.M. "Culture and Negotiation." *International Journal of Psychology 35*, no. 2 (April 2000), pp. 97–104.

- Tu, Y-T. "Cultural Characteristics and Negotiation Styles." *Journal of Economics and Behavioural Studies* 4, no. 5 (2012), pp. 297–306.

Books

- Ting-Toomey, S.; and J.G. Oetzel. *Managing Intercultural Conflict Effectively.* Thousand Oaks, CA: Sage, 2001.
- Varner, I.; and L. Beamer. *Intercultural Communication in the Global Workplace.* 5th ed. Boston, MA: McGraw Hill, 2010.
- Lewis, R. *When Teams Collide: Managing the International Team Successfully.* Boston, MA: Nicholas Brealey, 2012.
- Martin, J.N.; and T.K. Nakayama. *Intercultural Communication in Contexts.* 6th ed. Boston, MA: McGraw-Hill, 2012.
- Adler, N.J. *Leadership Insight.* New York, NY: Routledge, 2010.
- Hofstede, G.; G.J. Hofstede; and M. Michael. *Cultures and Organizations: Software for the Mind.* 3rd ed. New York, NY: McGraw-Hill, 2010.
- Trompenaars, F.; and C. Hampden-Turner. *Riding the Waves of Culture: Understanding Diversity in Global Business.* 3rd ed. New York, NY: McGraw Hill, 2011.
- Brake, T. *Where in the World is My Team?* Hoboken, NJ: John Wiley & Sons, 2008.
- Lewis, R. *When Teams Collide: Managing the International Team Successfully.* Boston, MA: Nicholas Brealey, 2012.
- Nemiro, J.; M.M. Beyerlein; L. Bradley.; and S. Beyerlein. *The Handbook of High Performance Virtual Teams: A Toolkit For Collaborating Across Boundaries.* San Francisco, CA: Jossey-Bass, 2010.
- Peterson, B. *Cultural Intelligence: A Guide to Working With People From Other Cultures.* Yarmouth, ME: Nicholas Brealey (Intercultural Press), 2004.
- Gudykunst, W.B.; and Y.Y. Kim. Communicating With Strangers: An Approach to Intercultural Communication. New York: McGraw-Hill, 1997.

- Chaney, L.H.; and J.S. Martin. *Intercultural Business Communication*. 4th ed. India: Dorling Kindersley Pvt. Ltd., 2011.
- Beamer, L.; and I. Varner. *Intercultural Communication in the Global Workplace*. 4th ed. New York: McGraw-Hill Irwin, 2008.
- Hall, E.T. *Beyond Culture*. New York: Doubleday, 1976.
- http://www.acis.pamplin.vt.edu/faculty/tegarden/5034/handouts/UI-CultureModels.pdf
- Smith, P.; M.H. Bond; and C. Kagitcibasi. "Fire and Ice: Testing a Model on Culture and Complex Problem Solving." In *Understanding Social Psychology Across Cultures: Living and Working in a Changing World*, eds. Guss, C.D. London: Sage, 2006.
- Victor, D.A. *International Business Communication*. New York, NY: Harper Collins Publishers Inc, 1992.
- Messner, W. *Working With India: The Softer Aspects of a Successful Collaboration with the Indian IT & BPO Industry*. Berlin and Heidelberg, Germany: Springer, 2010.
- Flaitz, J. *Understanding Your International Students: An Educational, Cultural, and Linguistic Guide*. Ann Arbor, MI: University of Michigan Press, 2003.
- Trosborg A. *Interlanguage Pragmatic: Requests, Complaints, and Apologies*. Berlin, Germany: Mouton de Gruyter, 1995.
- Hall, E.T. *Beyond Culture*. Garden City, NY: Doubleday, 1976.
- Fielding, M. *Effective Communication in Organisations: Preparing Messages That Communicate*. 3rd ed. Juta and Co. Pvt Ltd, 2006.
- Bartlett, C.A.; and S. Ghoshal. *Managing Across Borders*. Boston, MA: Harvard Business School Press, 1998.
- Chen, M. *Asian Management Systems: Chinese, Japanese, and Korean Styles of Business*. London and New York, NY: Routledge, 1995.
- Smith, K., Lindgren, I. & Granlund, R. (2007). Bridging Cultural Barriers to Collaborative Decision Making in On-Site Operations Coordination Centers. Final report to Räddningsverket, 2007. Report: LiU-IEI-R- -07/0002, Linköping university, Sweden.
- Fang, T. *Chinese Business Negotiating Style*. CA: Sage Publications, 1999.
- Martin, J.S.; and L.H. Chaney. *Global Business Etiquette*. Westport, CT: Praeger Publishers, 2006.

- Morrison, T.; W. Conaway; and G. Borden. *Kiss, Bow, or Shake Hands.* Avon, MA: Adams Media, 1994.

Additional Books

- Brynningsen, G. "Managing Expatriates on International Assignments." *Otago Management Graduate Review* 7, 2009.
- Löppönen, H. *Communication Challenges in an Expatriate Program, Case Company: IKEA Ltd* [Bachelor's Thesis Degree Programme in International Business]. 2012.
- Phonmang, K. *A Pilot Study on Cross Cultural Communication of Thai Expatriate Managers Working in Taiwan-Based Thai Organization* (Ref 1.23 Referred Paper). TAIWAN: Institute of International Workforce Education and Development, National Taiwan Normal University.
- Ishii, K. *The Effect of Cultural Differences in Communication and Feedback Styles on Employee: Adaptation to a Multinational Corporation (MNC)* (WCA Proceedings Paper). Bowling Green, KY: Western Kentucky University.
- Lee, H. *Adjustments in Inter-Cultural Communication of Expatriate and host National in Local Operation* [UNLV Theses/ Dissertations/Professional Papers/Capstones] (Paper 482). Las Vegas, NV: University of Nevada, 2010.
- Haghirian, P. *Does Culture Really Matter? Cultural Influences on the Knowledge Transfer Process within Multinational Corporations* [International Marketing and Management]. Vienna, Austria: Vienna University of Economics and Business Administration.
- Forssberg, S.; and S. Malm. *Internal Communication in an MNC: An Underestimated Key to Success* (Master Thesis No 2001-50) [International Business]. Graduate Business School, School of Economics and Commercial Law, Göteborg University, ISSN 1403-851X: Elanders Novum AB, 2001.
- Freeman, K.; S. Gopalan.; and J. Bailey. "Will the Acquisition Fail Due to Cultural Differences?" *Journal of Case Research in Business and Economics.*

- Chynoweth, C. "Dare to Try, the Indian Way." *The Sunday Times*, April 17, 2011. Times Newspapers Ltd.
- Gupta, M. "Euphoria Apart, the Merger is Half-Baked." *Economic Times*, June 27, 2006.
- *Putting the Shine Back Into Tata Steel by Prince Mathews Thomas.* April 15, 2013, India: Forbes. This article appeared in Forbes India Magazine of April 19, 2013.
- De Smedt, S.; and M.V. Hoey. "Integrating Steel Giants: An Interview With the Arcelor Mittal Post-Merger Managers," *Mckinsey Quarterly,* (Februrary 2008).
- *French Minister Threatens to Expel Arcelor Mittal,* 26 November 2012, www.bbc.com
- Bouwman, C.H.S. "The Role of Corporate Culture in Mergers & Acquisitions". In *Mergers and Acquisitions: Practices, Performance and Perspectives,* NOVA Science Publishers, May 2013.
- http://www.communicaid.com/i Cross-cultural training News Communicaid Helps Corus Integrate with Tata Steel
- Hoerr, A. *Keys to Guiding a Successful Merger or Acquisition: White Paper.* Champaign, IL: Serra Ventures, Inc, November 4, 2009.
- Holt, D. "How to Build an Iconic Brand." *Market Leader,* (Summer 2003), pp. 35–42.
- Schweiger, D.M.; and Y. Weber. "Strategies for Managing Human Resources During Mergers and Acquisitions: An Empirical Investigation." *Human Resource Planning* 12, no. 2 (June 1989), pp. 69.
- Hajro A.; and R. Baier. *In The Moderating Effect of Time on the Micro-Processes of Cross-Cultural Interactions in Multinational Teams,* Submission to the IACCM Conference, Vienna, 2009.
- Mattsson, M.; and S. Helsinki. *Gecos Report on Virtual Cross-Cultural Teams,* University of Technology, TAI Research Centre. Laboratory of Work Psychology and Leadership, 1998.
- Graham J.L.; and N.M. Lam. "The Chinese Negotiation." *Harvard Business Review,* (October 2003), p. 82.
- Cohen, R. Negotiating Across Cultures. 2nd Edition. Washington, D.C.: U.S. Institute of Peace, 1997. pp. 9–43; pp.215–226

Recommended Films

- Outsourced
- Gung Ho
- Bend it Like Beckham
- Shanghai Noon
- Jewel of the Nile
- The Last Samurai
- Rising Sun
- You Don't Mess with the Zohan
- Lost in Translation
- My Big Fat Greek Wedding

Index

OTHER TITLES IN THE CORPORATE COMMUNICATION COLLECTION

Debbie DuFrene, Stephen F. Austin State University, Editor

- *Managing Investor Relations: Strategies for Effective Communication* by Alexander Laskin
- *Managing Virtual Teams* by Debbie DuFrene and Carol Lehman
- *Corporate Communication: Tactical Guidelines for Strategic Practice* by Michael Goodman and Peter B. Hirsch
- *Communicating to Lead and Motivate* by William C. Sharbrough
- *Communication Strategies for Today's Managerial Leader* by Deborah Roebuck
- *Communication in Responsible Business: Strategies, Concepts, and Cases* by Roger N.Conaway and Oliver Laasch
- *Web Content: A Writer's Guide* by Janet Mizrahi
- *Intercultural Communication for Managers* by Michael B. Goodman
- *Today's Business Communication: A How-To Guide for the Modern Professional* by Jason L. Snyder and Robert Forbus
- *Fundamentals of Writing for Marketing and Public Relations: A Step-by-Step Guide for Quick and Effective Results* by Janet Mizrahi
- *Managerial Communication: Evaluating the Right Dose* by Johnson J. David
- *Leadership Talk: A Discourse Approach to Leader Emergence* by Robyn Walker and Jolanta Aritz

Announcing the Business Expert Press Digital Library

*Concise E-books Business Students Need
for Classroom and Research*

This book can also be purchased in an e-book collection by your library as
- a one-time purchase,
- that is owned forever,
- allows for simultaneous readers,
- has no restrictions on printing, and
- can be downloaded as PDFs from within the library community.

Our digital library collections are a great solution to beat the rising cost of textbooks. E-books can be loaded into their course management systems or onto students' e-book readers.

The **Business Expert Press** digital libraries are very affordable, with no obligation to buy in future years. For more information, please visit **www.businessexpertpress.com/librarians**. To set up a trial in the United States, please email **sales@businessexpertpress.com**.

www.ingramcontent.com/pod-product-compliance
Lightning Source LLC
Chambersburg PA
CBHW060611210326
41519CB00014B/3626